Reflections on Family, Faith, and Love

Through the Eyes of a Baby Boomer

Arthur Riley

© Copyrights 2025

Dedication

To My Wife, Vickie, My Partner In Our Adventure
Of Family, Faith, And Love!

Contents

Introduction	6
HEREDITY AND THE EARLY YEARS	**9**
What is a Baby Boomer?	10
The World through the Eyes of a Baby Boomer	15
The Family Chain	20
On the Banks of The Monocacy	27
16!	31
Tales of a Silver Tempest	36
FIRST KISS	40
The Gift	42
OCTOBER MOON	45
FAITH: THE MANDATORY INGREDIENT OF LIFE	**48**
Foundation of Faith	49
The Many Faces of God's Grace	53
Shadows and Sunlight	57
Christmas Is	61
Are We Listening?	66
Go Find Jesus	70
WHAT MAKES ME TICK	**74**
People + Relationships + Service	75
Pieces Create a Mosaic	79
People and Travel	83
Around the Next Bend	87
The Frosting of Life	89

Lady Liberty	93
THE CANYON SPEAKS	96
Magical Mountains	98
Shoebox in the Attic	100
Passing Memories	102
LOVE	**105**
Four Little Letters	106
Life of Love	108
An Invitation from God	110
My Special Angel	114
REFLECTIONS	**117**
Yesterday, Today, and Tomorrow	118
In the Rearview Mirror	121
The Future Must Start Today	126
Epilogue	132
Acknowledgements	136

INTRODUCTION

*"Memory is the diary that we all
carry about with us."*
— Oscar Wilde, Irish poet and playwright

Every life is a unique and one-of-a-kind journey, shaped by countless personal experiences, inherited traits, and relationships. Growing up in a bustling condominium community in New York City is an entirely different reality from being raised on an open ranch in Montana. These contrasting environments create distinct outlooks and temperaments, influencing the very fabric of who we are.

Our DNA serves as a biological blueprint, an unbroken thread that links us to generations before us. At the same time, relationships act as the scaffolding of our character, shaping our beliefs, fueling our ambitions, and molding our identities in ways we often fail to recognize.

The influence of these elements—nature, nurture, and connection—can be debated endlessly. Yet, one truth remains constant: it is the people around us who color the canvas of our existence. Every interaction, whether a fleeting exchange on a street corner or a lifelong companionship, adds its own shade to the portrait of our lives.

Some argue that our destinies are predetermined, as if we are pawns moving across a chessboard with no control over the game. I believe otherwise. Life, to me, is an ever-changing interplay of choices and chance—a series of crossroads where decisions and coincidences intersect to shape our path. The people we meet, whether through deep bonds or brief encounters, influence the trajectory of our lives. And when all these moments—big and small—are layered together, they define who we ultimately become.

From the very first moments with our parents, our lives take shape through an unending cycle of growth and evolution. Childhood molds us. Adolescence expands our horizons, introducing new voices and fresh perspectives. With adulthood comes an ever-widening circle of connections—friends who become family, mentors who leave indelible marks, colleagues who teach us lessons, and acquaintances who alter the course of a single day.

No matter their depth or duration, every relationship leaves a trace. These interactions carve our values, nurture our interests, and fortify the beliefs that guide us. Within this inner core, cherished memories take root, becoming part of the essence of who we are.

What makes these memories so remarkable is that they are rarely deliberate creations. Instead, they arrive like sparks—born from laughter, shaped by love, or tempered by loss—ignited by forces beyond our control. Some are filled with joy, others tinged with sorrow, yet all of them reflect the people and events that collided in the mystery of a single moment.

Years later, those same memories often resurface unbidden. A melody drifting through the air, a photograph glimpsed in passing, or even a faint scent on a breeze can transport us back in time. In those moments, the past breathes again, reminding us not only of who we were, but how far we have come.

Why do certain memories cling to us more than others? Why does a brief conversation with a stranger sometimes leave a deeper mark than years spent with someone familiar? Why do friendships from decades ago suddenly drift into consciousness without warning? And why are some relationships—sometimes brief, sometimes enduring—so profoundly influential in shaping the people we become?

The answers to these questions may forever elude us. But what I do know is this: the memories contained in these pages hold clues. They were forged through countless interactions, in places near and far, across moments both ordinary and extraordinary. Each one has helped define my identity and has guided the evolution of my philosophies.

This collection is my attempt to preserve a fragment of that journey—to share a glimpse of my life with my family and offer insights into the person I have grown to be. Through these stories, poems, and letters, I hope to capture not only the details of my experiences, but the essence of what they meant to me.

I have chosen to omit specific names out of respect for privacy. While including them might have added vividness, my goal was never to embarrass anyone. If I have inadvertently done so, or if you find yourself absent from a story you expected to see, please know that it was never intentional.

My hope is that these recollections will make you smile unexpectedly, or stir a cherished memory of your own.

To my children and grandchildren: may these words help you understand the man behind the name. And when you share these stories with future generations, let them know who POPS truly was—not just as a name on a family tree, but as a life fully lived.

Arthur Riley

2025

Heredity and the Early Years

What is a Baby Boomer?

"Posterity! You will never know how much it costs the present generation to preserve your freedom! I hope you will make good use of it."

— John Adams, Second President of the United States

The term Baby Boomer refers to children born between 1946 and 1964, during a remarkable population increase that followed World War II. This generation, spanning two full decades, was shaped by a unique blend of historical events that influenced their perspectives, values, and their impact on society.

Boomers, born in the immediate postwar years, grew up in the shadow of the so-called Greatest Generation. Their parents were men and women who had endured the Great Depression, responded to the attack on Pearl Harbor in 1941, and persevered until victory was secured in 1945. Military fathers and unmarried men often spent years overseas, while women stepped into factories and shipyards, assembling airplanes, radios, and other essential equipment. Their resilience and sacrifices laid the foundation upon which Baby Boomers were raised.

Even before the war, the Great Depression had left deep scars. Those fortunate enough to find work had little disposable income, while farmers relied on the land, laboring from dawn to dusk to provide for their families. My grandfather Riley, for example, picked cherries for six cents a quart and planted corn for twenty-five cents a day. It was not uncommon for families to move from town to town in search of work. These hardships shaped the worldview of the generation that would later raise the Boomers, and those struggles inevitably influenced the children themselves.

When the war ended, families turned their attention to rebuilding. Fathers returned home eager to restore a sense of normalcy, and many couples sought to start families of their own. Providing for a household often required six-and-a-half workdays each week, sometimes supplemented by a second job. Idle time was scarce, with household chores consuming most evenings. Sundays were devoted to church, rest, and extended family gatherings.

This atmosphere fostered a culture of resilience and discipline. A strong work ethic, loyalty to community, respect for authority, and a renewed emphasis on education became defining features of early Baby Boomer upbringing. Traditional gender roles were reinforced, conservative financial habits were valued, and homeownership became a goal that symbolized stability. Above all, there was a widespread belief in American exceptionalism, one that guided the optimism of the era.

The world soon shifted again. The Korean War in the early 1950s disrupted families just as they were beginning to settle. Unlike World War II, this conflict entered American homes in a new way: through television. Families watched wartime footage on small black-and-white screens, through storefront displays, or at local theaters before the main feature. For some children, including myself, the consequences were immediate and personal. At five years old, I struggled to comprehend why my friend and neighbor was growing up without a father.

By the late 1950s, television had become more than a novelty—it was woven into the rhythm of daily life. Children hurried to living rooms to watch Howdy Doody, Saturday morning cartoons, and the endless stream of cowboy westerns starring figures like Roy Rogers and Gene Autry. I can still recall sitting cross-legged in front of the television, eagerly waiting for Howdy Doody, Winky Dink, or the thrilling adventures of Sky King.

Television also shaped entertainment in other ways. Many sitcoms featured performers who had once thrived on the Vaudeville stage. Their sharp comedic timing and well-polished routines transitioned seamlessly to television, making them household names.

The mid-1960s introduced a new milestone: color broadcasts. The vivid hues of color television transformed the way families experienced entertainment, replacing the starkness of black and white with a brighter, more immediate sense of presence.

Television soon influenced politics as well. The first televised presidential debate, between John F. Kennedy and Richard Nixon, captured the nation's attention and altered the way Americans evaluated their leaders. Kennedy's youthful energy and polished style offered a striking contrast to the steadier presence of Dwight Eisenhower and the more somber Nixon.

The assassination of Kennedy in November 1963 left an indelible scar. Americans of every age could recall precisely where they were when they heard the shocking news—whether it was a mother in her kitchen or a sixteen-year-old student, like me, sitting in an Algebra II classroom. That weekend in Dallas shook the nation and altered the course of politics. Congressional leaders such as Gerald Ford, Everett Dirksen, and Henry Jackson emerged as statesmen while the towering influence of Lyndon Johnson and Sam Rayburn guided policy.

By 1974, the first resignation of a sitting U.S. president further tested the country's stability. The years that followed were marked by uncertainty until Ronald Reagan emerged as a figure of reassurance. With warmth, confidence, and an ability to connect with ordinary Americans, Reagan helped restore a sense of optimism while easing Cold War anxieties.

The 1950s and 1960s were defined by transformation. The Civil Rights movement exposed injustices long ignored, while the Vietnam War fractured the nation along generational and ideological lines. Technology accelerated at an unprecedented pace, with the invention of the microchip paving the way for air travel, computers, and space exploration.

The Mercury Seven astronauts—Alan Shepard, John Glenn, and their peers—ignited imaginations across the globe, their missions culminating in the Apollo program. Millions watched in awe as Neil Armstrong took humankind's first steps on the moon in 1969, his words echoing across living rooms worldwide.

At the same time, automobiles became symbols of freedom and identity for the Baby Boom generation. The sleek Ford Mustang, the raw power of the Pontiac GTO, and the elegance of the Chevrolet Corvette were not merely cars but cultural statements. They embodied independence, adventure, and the boundless possibilities of youth. For many, cruising down a wide-open highway with the wind rushing through the windows was the purest expression of postwar optimism.

Baby Boomers have lived through prosperity and upheaval, progress and disillusionment. They reshaped consumer culture, challenged political institutions, and pushed the boundaries of personal freedom. While I cannot claim to have been a driving force in these transformations, the experiences remain deeply embedded in my memory.

Our lives are remembered not only by world events but also by the people we meet, the places we hold dear, and the moments we share. Baby Boomers entered adolescence during the vibrant and turbulent 1960s—a decade that challenged racial divides, cultural conventions, and political loyalties. By the late 1960s and early 1970s, they were marrying, raising children, and stepping into civic responsibility.

Now, as many of this generation enter retirement, their influence persists. From the moon landing to civil rights, from Vietnam to economic reform, Baby Boomers carry with them lessons from a lifetime of extraordinary change. Their imprint remains visible in society today and will continue to shape the decades ahead.

The World through the Eyes of a Baby Boomer

"And those who were seen dancing were thought to be crazy by those who could not hear the music."
— *Friedrich Nietzsche, German Philosopher*

Life is a miracle. God places us where our talents are most needed, among people who benefit from our abilities, or in situations where we can grow in character and stature. Each of us has the chance to carve out a meaningful place in the world—one that leaves behind a lasting legacy and memories that endure.

As a baby boomer, I was fortunate to live in a time and place that encouraged my aspirations and allowed me to take part in one of the most dynamic periods of modern history. My experiences do not mirror those of all baby boomers, yet they reflect the journey of a significant portion of my generation. We witnessed sweeping changes, endured profound challenges, experienced cultural transformations, and saw remarkable progress—all while anchoring our lives in relationships that gave us purpose and grounding.

The Cold War shaped much of our early lives, looming like a shadow over our childhoods with its constant threat of nuclear war. We followed international conflicts in Korea and Vietnam with unease, watched the Berlin Wall physically divide not only a city but a nation, and learned to measure the world through the lens of tension and suspicion. The decolonization of Africa, the rise of political power from the People's Republic of China, and the ongoing instability in South America, Southeast Asia, and the Middle East further impressed upon us the fragility of global balance.

For many, these events crystallized during the Vietnam War. The conflict was a crucible that tested the nation's conscience and redefined generational identity. Americans questioned the wisdom of waging war in a distant and culturally unfamiliar region. The press, emboldened by its influence, became politically vocal, challenging government policies with a newfound audacity. The country was split—patriots who saw honor in the fight stood against critics who questioned its morality and necessity. In the middle of this ideological battlefield stood the soldiers themselves, courageous young men and women who carried out their duty despite the chaos swirling around them. Their bravery became a symbol of sacrifice, even as the nation wrestled with its divided soul.

Equally transformative were the cultural battles fought at home. The Civil Rights Movement redefined American society, forcing long-ignored questions into the open. Baby boomers were among the first to witness school desegregation firsthand, often caught between respect for adults in their lives and the dawning realization that segregation was unjust. By the 1960s, African American children were entering classrooms once reserved for white students, while Black college students increasingly exercised their right to choose institutions that best fit their ambitions.

As access to education grew, so too did cultural influence. Music, sports, and entertainment offered new opportunities for representation. Motown's music transcended race and became the soundtrack of a generation. Black performers appeared more prominently on television, in films, and on concert stages.

Athletes like Jackie Robinson, whose courage broke racial barriers in baseball, inspired a wave of participation across professional sports.

Communities themselves were changing in form and rhythm. The postwar years brought rapid suburban growth, as families sought quieter lives away from crowded cities. This migration reshaped the nation's identity. The once-dominant agricultural economy faded, replaced by an industrial and suburban model of living that emphasized new comforts and consumer lifestyles.

For baby boomers, adolescence opened a world of opportunity. Teenagers explored extracurricular activities, worked part-time jobs, and formed friendships that stretched beyond the confines of family farms or small towns. Main Streets in places like Westminster came alive with young workers—teens folding clothes in department stores, serving food at diners, dishing ice cream at drug store soda fountains, or bagging groceries at the corner market.

These jobs were more than a source of spending money. They taught responsibility, punctuality, and resourcefulness. They also nurtured community bonds, showing us that every role, no matter how small, contributed to something larger. The underlying lesson was clear: with discipline and determination, prosperity was not only possible but within reach.

A newfound love of the automobile further defined this mobility. Cars meant freedom—family vacations stretched farther, commutes grew longer, and teenagers experienced independence in ways previous generations could not. The Riley family, like many others, embraced this culture of travel, driving by station wagon to California in 1956 and to the Canadian Rockies in 1965. By 1964, even teenagers were traveling by air, as I did when I flew to Dallas, Texas, for the Key Club International Convention.

Consumerism blossomed alongside this new mobility. Products designed to make life easier filled homes across America. The telephone is perhaps the best example of this transformation. In the years immediately following World War II, calling required an operator to manually connect lines. Many households shared "party lines," with neighbors often overhearing conversations. The arrival of dial telephones offered independence, while push-button phones in the 1960s sped up communication and gave users direct control. What once seemed futuristic — the idea of carrying a personal phone — became reality within a generation, rendering payphones nearly obsolete.

Technology also claimed its share of casualties. Slide rules, typewriters, encyclopedias, and black-and-white televisions, once fixtures of daily life, faded into obsolescence. In their place came pocket calculators, color television, and, eventually, the computer chip.

The space race highlighted this technological shift. When the Soviet Union launched Sputnik in 1957, it ignited global competition that carried us from Alan Shepard's first suborbital flight to John Glenn's orbit of Earth. The tragedies, such as the Apollo 1 fire, did not halt progress but strengthened determination, ultimately culminating in Neil Armstrong's unforgettable first steps on the moon in 1969. For our generation, the impossible became possible, and today's children continue to dream of journeys beyond Earth.

Technology also transformed everyday business. When I began working in a pharmacy in 1963, all records were handwritten and transactions were either cash or check. Over the years, I watched as credit card systems, insurance billing, and computerized record-keeping revolutionized retail. By the early 1980s, Washington Heights Pharmacy proudly installed the second computerized pharmacy system in Maryland, a milestone that underscored how quickly our world was changing.

Consumer voices shaped these innovations. Shoppers demanded products that saved time and simplified life—TV dinners, transistor radios, and eventually microwaves. Yet, as some conveniences rose, others disappeared: green stamps, drive-in theaters, home milk deliveries, and five-and-dime stores. Women, in particular, guided these trends. Long the stewards of household budgets, they expanded their influence into the workplace and the broader consumer economy, all while sustaining traditions like church attendance that grounded family life.

Sports grew in parallel with consumerism. Little League, high school games, and college athletics flourished, while professional sports became powerful industries. Baseball spread from the Midwest to the Pacific Coast, securing its place as the national pastime. Television expanded the reach of all sports—ABC's "Wide World of Sports" and extensive Olympic coverage brought global competition into American living rooms. The 1980 Winter Olympics, with the U.S. hockey team's victory over the Soviet Union, was etched forever in memory as the "Miracle on Ice."

From these experiences, baby boomers learned resilience, determination, and the value of community. We came to cherish human connections and developed an enduring spirit of self-reliance. Friendships, family, and community ties forged in youth remain the cornerstones of our lives.

Looking back, I recognize the privilege of having grown up during this extraordinary period. My memories stretch from sock hops to senior proms, from the rise of rock and roll to the soulful notes of the blues. They encompass victories and setbacks, fleeting romances and lifelong commitments.

Those memories ultimately led me to a magnificent wife, a family I am immensely proud of, and a life filled with experiences I never imagined but forever treasure.

The Family Chain

"How strange is the lot of us mortals! Each of us is here for a brief sojourn, for what purpose we know not, though sometimes we sense it. But we know from daily life that we exist for other people — first of all, for whose smiles and well-being our own happiness depends."
— Albert Einstein, Theoretical Physicist

The scent of ripe apples hanging heavy in the air is one of the most familiar fragrances of my life. It carries me back to autumn days spent driving through the orchards near Biglerville, Pennsylvania — a place that feels like an extension of my very being. Each October, when the orchards blaze with color, a certain spell settles over me.

My ancestors were among the European settlers who brought apple trees across the Atlantic Ocean, and their roots — like the trees themselves — took hold in this land. The apple industry they helped to establish now produces more than five million bushels annually, a living testament to their perseverance and foresight. Yet, their efforts were not confined to apples alone. They cultivated cherries, peaches, and plums, each harvest a reflection of their determination to thrive in a new world.

My connection to the Riley history is anchored in the countless hours I have spent exploring the region and attending family reunions. Each visit reinforces my belonging to that unbroken family chain stretching back generations, with links extending to Ireland, England, Germany, and the Alsace region of France. The stories of those who came before me are not distant records; they live within me, shaping my memories and a sense of identity.

My earliest memories, like most people's, revolve around family. Families differ in size, character, and history, yet I consider myself fortunate to have been born in the mid-twentieth century, just after World War II. Fathers were returning home from service in Europe, Africa, the Pacific, India, the Aleutian Islands, and "stateside" posts.

My father rarely spoke of his time with the U.S. Navy Seabees in Hawaii, Guam, and Enewetak. Silence, I came to understand, was his way of moving forward. On his return, like many veterans, he was determined to reclaim the time the war had stolen. He worked tirelessly to build a good life for my mother, my sisters, and me, determined that we should never taste the hardships he had endured during the Depression.

When I entered the world in 1947, an older sister was already there to greet me. Two more sisters followed in 1950 and 1954. Together, we grew up under the guidance of a father who was a gifted salesman and a mother whose devotion to her children was the backbone of our home. She supervised a household that ran with quiet efficiency, and she brought creativity to every meal she placed on the table. The lessons absorbed from both of them — his drive and her devotion — formed the foundation for our future successes.

Among my most cherished recollections are those of my grandparents. My first date-specific memory is of playing in a sandbox with my maternal grandmother, Myrtle. Though our time together was brief, her warm smile and gentle presence left a lasting imprint. I loved those autumn afternoons at her house in 1949. That date stays clear in my mind because the very next spring, in April 1950, I stood in a funeral home at her viewing. She had lost her battle with diabetes and its cardiac complications. At three years old, I could not comprehend what a funeral meant—only that something precious had slipped away.

After her passing, I spent more time with my grandfather Scott, perhaps as much his way of easing loneliness as it was nurturing me. I was named after Arthur Scott and my paternal grandfather, Norman Riley—a heritage I have always carried with pride.

Some of my fondest days were those fishing trips with Grandpa Scott to Deal Island on Maryland's Eastern Shore. In the early years, we crossed the Chesapeake Bay by ferry; later, the Chesapeake Bay Bridge shortened the journey. We would cast our lines off Piney Island at dawn or dusk, baiting hooks with peeler crabs and waiting for the jolt of a bite, the surge of excitement as a "rock" fish bent the line. In the fall, we boarded a larger boat to bottom-fish for sea trout in Tangier Sound.

Dinner afterward was always a celebration of the sea—platters of fresh rockfish, trout, croakers, or Maryland blue crabs. Each meal was a feast of flavor and memory.

Saturdays brought a different kind of tradition—"pancake mornings." My cousin and I would watch, wide-eyed, as Grandpa mixed batter, poured it onto the griddle, and flipped golden circles that we eagerly smothered with butter and maple syrup. Between mouthfuls, he would share fragments of his philosophy on life. Much of the detail has blurred with time, but the essence of his words stayed with me, forming the groundwork for deeper conversations I came to value during college visits home.

As I later faced the trials of running my own business, my admiration for my grandfather's accomplishments deepened. His career began at Dennison Manufacturing in New England. By the mid-1920s, he moved his young family—wife, two sons, and a daughter—to Illinois for a superintendent position at a farm machinery manufacturer. Yet, his entrepreneurial spirit could not be confined.

In the heart of the Depression, Arthur and Myrtle Scott chose Westminster, Maryland, to establish Beacon Steel Products Company, a manufacturing business serving farmers across the mid-Atlantic. Against the odds, the company thrived, sustaining not only his family but also those of his children. As his first grandson, I occasionally worked in the plant, loading trucks as a teenager. Years later, I came to appreciate the words of former employees who spoke with respect about his fair leadership, concern for his workers, and vision for the business.

My education extended well beyond what I learned from my maternal grandfather. My paternal grandparents, Grammie and Pap-Pap, imparted their own form of wisdom. Their philosophy was simple yet profound: each grandchild was unique and deserved to be treated as such. Their love showed in countless ways, whether providing my older sister with a temporary home so she could start school early, or finding time to read stories, play dominoes, and share the rhythms of their rural life.

Self-sufficiency had been bred into them during World War I and the Depression. Their days revolved around raising chickens, slopping hogs, and tending Grammie's carefully ordered garden of asparagus, zucchini, and other vegetables. Each season carried its own duties. Spring brought baby chicks arriving in the mail and seed catalogs promising new harvests. Summer meant strawberries piled on sundaes and the taste of deep red cherries plucked from the trees in the side yard. Autumn was the time of preparation: grapes pressed into juice, jars of vegetables sealed for winter, and the annual butchering of two hogs in November.

Yet their home was more than work. It was alive with scents that etched themselves into memory. The smokehouse carried a sharp, lingering tang after hams and bacon were cured. The farmhouse kitchen greeted visitors with the warmth of the wood stove, which Grammie knew how to command with practiced ease as she baked cakes and cookies for her grandchildren. But the most indelible aroma was the Sunday dinner spread: crispy fried chicken, mashed potatoes bathed in gravy, and thick slices of home-baked bread dripping with molasses.

The most important lessons I learned from my grandparents were respect for a day's work, the centrality of family, and the responsibility of civic understanding. Both of them came from humble beginnings and spent their lives working with steady hands and steady hearts.

My Grammie's work was never truly finished. She managed the small farmette with quiet determination, tending to animals, gardens, and household tasks that stretched from dawn until dusk. My grandfather Riley shouldered several jobs to keep the family afloat—he labored at the grist mill, stood long hours as a security guard, worked as a carpenter, picked fruit in the nearby orchards, and still found the energy to plant crops of his own. His ethic was simple: work was not only survival, it was dignity.

Grandfather Scott, in contrast, walked a different but equally demanding road. While working full-time, he pursued and earned an engineering degree. Even then, he did not step into success without obligation—he carried the weight of caring for his widowed mother, never wavering in his duty. His experiences gave him an intimate knowledge of what it meant to build and maintain a successful business. That understanding became the foundation of his own endeavors.

Each grandparent demonstrated the importance of family in their own way. They made sure there were visits to cousins, aunts, and uncles. They upheld traditions like attending annual family reunions. And most memorably, they gave us, their grandchildren, the gift of their time—stories told at kitchen tables, laughter shared while rocking on the front porch, and lessons slipped into everyday conversations.

Pap-Pap, especially, exhibited his commitment to civic understanding. Each morning, he opened the daily newspaper with care, and after completion at 9 AM he tuned the radio to the distinctive voice declaring, "This is Paul Harvey in Chicago." Those routines weren't mere habits—they were his way of staying connected with the wider world. Pap-Pap and Grandpa were always ready to talk about current events, community happenings, and what those events meant for ordinary families like ours.

Their teachings were consistent: honesty was non-negotiable, individual responsibility was expected, and personal integrity was the measure of a life well lived. Abandoning any of these principles simply wasn't an option.

Additional tales of my relationships with them could easily fill many more pages. Yet, what matters most is the event that began our family's story: the meeting of my mother and father. It was August 1940, at the Forest and Stream Club, where they first crossed paths. Their courtship blossomed quickly, culminating in marriage in November 1941—just one month before the attack on Pearl Harbor would change the world.

Through the years, my sisters were my constant companions, always loving and supportive. Together we created a trove of memorable moments, strengthened by the steady guidance of our parents and grandparents. Their influence shaped us in ways both seen and unseen, and I can only hope our lives stand as a living tribute to theirs. Even so, I sometimes wonder if I absorbed enough of their wisdom, if I carried forward as much as I should have.

Life on this rock we call Earth is but a brief stay, yet what we do during that stay leaves an imprint—on those who came before us and those who will follow. On a clear night, far from the wash of city lights, the vastness of the universe reveals itself. The stars scatter across the heavens, each with its own intensity, while meteors blaze suddenly across the darkness, unannounced and fleeting.

In the east, the moon climbs slowly above the horizon, bathing the land in silver. The heavens seem almost within reach, as if one could stretch out a hand and touch eternity. Then, a shift of the eye finds the brilliance of Polaris, the North Star, steady and faithful. As the hours pass, the slow rotation of the stars around it unveils the natural order of the skies.

When I gaze at that order, I find myself reflecting on my ancestors, on the family values they entrusted to me, and on my role in carrying them forward. The same hand of God that set the planets into orbit and bound the Milky Way together is the hand that has guided generations, bringing families to life and ensuring their continuance.

My generation, like those before and after, occupies this world only for a moment in the vast continuum of time. But in that moment, we create memories, we strengthen bonds, and we leave behind legacies. Those memories, both tender and profound, flow into the family chain, carrying the past into the future.

On the Banks of The Monocacy

"Let us be grateful to the people who make us happy; they are the charming gardeners who make our souls blossom."
– Marcel Proust, French Novelist

The Monocacy River, whose name means "the river with many bends," carves its winding course through Maryland farmland, its curves reflecting the meandering paths of my youth. When I sit on a familiar rock beside its peaceful waters, I am transported back to sun-drenched summers along this river—to the place we simply called "camp." Though I am an adult now, the riverbanks still hold vivid snapshots of those carefree days, etched as sharply as if they happened yesterday.

This scenic stretch of the Monocacy, a tributary of the Potomac, became the backdrop for memories shared with several families during my formative summers. Six to eight families gathered there, bringing along nearly twenty children, our ages separated by only a handful of years. On the riverbank, "camp" was made up of simple two-room cabins, each one filled with laughter, chatter, and the occasional squabble. Over several weeks each summer, we built friendships that not only endured but flourished into lifelong bonds. Looking back, I realize it wasn't merely the setting that made it extraordinary. It was the rhythm of life we shared, and the way adults and youth lived side by side in a rare harmony that helped shape who we became.

It was the late 1950s and early 1960s—a world untroubled by computer games, electronic gadgets, or even basic three-channel television, which had no place at camp. Days began with hearty breakfasts—pancakes piled high, crisp bacon, and mugs of hot chocolate that steamed comfort into cool mornings. Chores were dispatched quickly—beds made, dishes washed, floors swept—because no one wanted to be the last one ready for the day's adventures.

The Monocacy itself was our constant companion and playground. We swam for hours, challenged each other to races, and held breath-holding contests beneath the surface. An old Navy raft anchored mid-river became both our fortress and our stage. Girls declared themselves "queens" while boys plotted playful revolts, our childhood dramas unfolding on those sun-warmed planks. As we grew older, our games matured into spirited water volleyball matches and improvised competitions that stretched late into the day.

Canoeing revealed another side of the river. Two or three of us would paddle upstream, pulling onto small islands or scrambling up rocky outcroppings that beckoned like secret fortresses. Fishing offered a quieter rhythm. With bamboo poles and red-and-white bobbers, we sat on the bank, waiting for a tug on the line, the stillness broken only by the river's current and the occasional dragonfly skimming across the surface.

Yet the river was more than water and games. It was a keeper of confidences. Under the canopy of stars, small groups and tentative couples shared hushed conversations that reached far beyond childhood. We spoke of college plans, uncertain futures, first stirrings of love, and the mysteries of adulthood. Those riverside talks—innocent yet profound—helped us begin to understand who we were becoming. Though we did not recognize it then, the moonlit confessions and laughter shaped our sense of the world.

Onshore, bicycles were our steeds, carrying us along winding backroads or into spirited races through camp. When energy shifted toward quieter pursuits, we poured ourselves into creativity. Plays were written and staged with comic flair, water carnivals filled the river with spectacle, and a makeshift circus saw the youngest children proudly parading as elephants and lions. The shows may have lacked polish, but they brimmed with enthusiasm. Older kids took the lead, guiding the younger ones, teaching us lessons in collaboration, compromise, and leadership. Parents sat in folding chairs, our eager audience, paying admission with dimes and quarters. Those coins soon turned into dripping ice cream cones from the general store—Neapolitan, a safe choice, though I still recall the sticky sweetness of chocolate marshmallow and the delicate flavor of peach in season.

No matter the day's adventure, by five o'clock we knew to expect the smoky aroma of charcoal signaling supper. Dinner was a communal feast: platters of fried chicken, sizzling hamburgers and hot dogs, or thick steaks from a local butcher. Side dishes—potato salad, coleslaw, baked beans—were set out in abundance. On special nights, Maryland blue crabs steamed in spice appeared on the table. I remember learning how to "pick" them properly, cracking shells to savor the tender backfin meat. Sweet corn, pulled from nearby fields and still warm from the sun, rounded out those summer indulgences.

Evenings carried their own magic. Softball games erupted, laughter echoing as adults misjudged fly balls or were tagged out by swift-footed kids. Hide-and-seek stretched into twilight, the trees, barns, and ravines transforming into an endless maze. Darkness brought new rhythms—dances in the clubhouse with stacks of 45s spinning, half chosen by the kids, half reserved for the adults who claimed the floor after curfew. On quieter nights, the click of cards hitting a wooden table filled the cabins as Michigan Poker battles raged for bragging rights. And sometimes, piling into cars for the drive-in movies, we didn't care what was showing — it was the adventure that mattered.

Amid these treasured memories, two shadows linger. One is a quiet regret: my children and grandchildren will never know this kind of carefree summer, untouched by screens and distractions. Their memories will be different, shaped by another era, but I hope just as sweet. The second shadow is personal — the memory of a girl from our group, my age, who died unexpectedly during college. We never had the chance to reminisce about our shared summers, but her smile remains etched in my mind.

Millions of gallons of water have flowed past camp since those days, carrying time forward like the current itself. The "camp kids," now grown, sometimes reunite, sharing laughter and stories that roll as easily as the river's flow. When I return to my rock on the Monocacy, the water whispers back fragments of our youth, reminding me of the bonds we forged on its banks. The ripples reflect not only the faces of who we were, but the enduring truth that those summers, and the friendships born there, are treasures time cannot erase.

Today, our numbers are fewer, but the memories remain unbroken. To have been part of that circle, to be a graduate of "camp," is a privilege I carry with quiet pride.

16!

"It takes courage to grow up and become who you really are."
— E. E. Cummings, American Poet, Essayist

"Sixteen Reasons" and "Sixteen Candles" remind us of the magic and milestones of turning sixteen. It is an age wedged between childhood and adulthood, brimming with change and a rising sense of independence. While parents often recognize that true maturity is still a long way off, a sixteen-year-old is convinced they are already an adult—especially with the freedom that comes with a driver's license.

My first fifteen years were shaped by a strong network of parents, family, friends, neighbors, Sunday School teachers, and educators who guided me through those early seasons of life. I was fortunate to be part of a community deeply invested in helping maturing baby boomers find their way. They offered stability, safety, opportunities for learning—both inside and outside the classroom—and a wide range of recreational experiences.

For me, sixteen was a year of new beginnings. It demanded more complex decisions, opened doors to greater opportunities, and introduced adventures that tested my independence. It was also a time when painful lessons in relationships began to shape my values and deepen my understanding of responsibility.

This pivotal year strongly influenced how I approached adulthood. One of the most important changes was in academics. In elementary and junior high, school often felt like a routine I simply endured; recess was far more appealing than homework. My grades were acceptable, but I lacked real motivation. That began to shift in early high school when my studies suddenly felt more relevant. I developed a genuine interest in biology, chemistry, and history, and teachers seemed more approachable. Elective courses expanded my world, showing me possibilities I had not considered before.

Music became another formative outlet. Being elected drum major of the "Owl" Marching Band gave me the chance to lead, while also nurturing a lifelong appreciation for a wide variety of musical styles. My participation in Key Club introduced me to service and the broader Kiwanis family. Those early experiences planted the seeds of volunteerism that would grow into a lasting commitment throughout my life.

Yet, as significant as academics and service were, they were often overshadowed by what I came to think of as the two "D's": driving and dating.

Shortly after my birthday, I traded in my trusty two-wheeled bicycle for the motorized independence of a car. With that freedom, I could attend carnivals, movies, school events, concerts, and parties. On many Saturday nights, our group of friends gathered at one another's homes—dancing to records, playing games, and enjoying food provided by watchful parents. Their hospitality had an unspoken purpose: to keep us off the streets and ensure they knew exactly where their children were.

Purchasing my first car unlocked the second "D," dating. That car became my passport into a new world of adventure—sometimes thrilling, sometimes nerve-racking. One summer evening, while driving home from a carnival, a sudden thunderstorm knocked out my windshield wipers. Arriving home late, I faced my father's pointed questions. Fortunately for me, the wipers still refused to work when he asked for a demonstration.

Another time, an early October snowfall arrived during a school hootenanny. I had to drive thirteen miles on slick, unfamiliar roads to take my date home. Every mile filled me with apprehension, yet the experience taught me caution and control. One of the most memorable trips of that year was to Atlantic City, where I met my parents at the Kiwanis International Convention. It was my first long-distance drive, and it boosted my confidence behind the wheel. Exploring the city and witnessing my first major fireworks display off the Steel Pier made the journey unforgettable.

With driving and dating came the sobering reality of money. Car insurance, gasoline, maintenance, tires, and dating expenses quickly added up. I wanted to play high school basketball, but balancing those costs with the time commitment the sport required seemed impossible. After much thought, I made the difficult choice to set basketball aside and take on a part-time job.

That search led me to the local Rexall Drug Store, where I earned 85 cents an hour. My responsibilities were varied: stocking shelves, cleaning, delivering prescriptions, and working the soda fountain before and after school. At the time, I had no idea that this small step would lead to a lifelong career in pharmacy spanning more than fifty years. (One early lesson in responsibility came when I had to open a checking account just to write my first check — to the Internal Revenue Service.)

Independence also changed how relationships developed. Adults in the community began to treat me differently, asking for my opinions and expecting me to consider theirs. Having a job seemed to raise the level of respect they offered.

Family connections deepened as well. My visits to Grammie Riley's farm were filled with lasting memories — gathering eggs, helping with chickens, or watching the hard work of hog butchering. No visit was complete without savoring her Sunday fried chicken dinners, served with freshly baked bread. I often wondered which cake or cookies would be waiting for me that day. As I grew older, lighthearted games of dominoes were gradually replaced with conversations about the importance of education. I wish I had cherished more of those talks, absorbing her practical wisdom. I also wish she had lived long enough to see me graduate from pharmacy school.

Both of my grandfathers shaped me in different but equally profound ways. Arthur Scott, the businessman, often spoke about the rewards and challenges of owning and managing a business. His lessons on treating people well and maintaining personal integrity became cornerstones of how I approached leadership later in life. I especially treasured the times I visited his office when home from college—lessons not found in textbooks, but essential for real-world success.

Norman Riley, my other grandfather, offered a different kind of guidance. Despite limited formal education, he was a skilled mathematician, a voracious reader, and deeply interested in history, politics, and world events. His values—truth, honesty, family, and hard work—were forged through the trials of two world wars, the Great Depression, and the demanding rhythms of orchard farming. His wisdom still echoes in my thoughts. At sixteen, I did not fully appreciate the depth of what he shared, though now I wish I had.

Not all relationships at sixteen were joyful. Two heartaches remain vivid: the loss of my beloved dog and the sting of first love. Lassie, our collie, had been my companion from my third birthday until she passed away at thirteen. She was more than a pet—she was playmate, protector, and comfort. Making the decision to end her suffering was one of the hardest moments of my young life.

The other ache came when my first serious girlfriend abruptly ended our relationship without explanation. That sudden ending left a wound that lingered far longer than I expected.

Ultimately, sixteen was a thrilling, formative year. For me, as for so many others, it was the foundation on which much of my adult life was built—a year alive with lessons, joys, challenges, and memories that continue to shape who I am.

Tales of a Silver Tempest

"Memory is the diary that we all carry about with us."
— Oscar Wilde, Irish Writer

"Tempest." I am not the raging kind, nor a tempest in a teacup, but a 1962 Pontiac—compact, sturdy, a bundle of steel and chrome built for the open road. My journey began in the clamor of a Detroit assembly plant, where the thunder of rivets, the hiss of welding torches, and the pounding rhythm of machinery created a symphony of industry. From there, I became a wanderer, passed from hand to hand, until fate deposited me on a modest used car lot in Westminster, Maryland.

My so-called crime? I was surrendered in exchange for a gleaming, showroom-perfect Corvette—a cruel trade that left me sitting in its shadow, my modest silhouette overlooked.

The autumn of 1963 was a lonely season. I sat idle as the weeks dragged by, my tires yearning to touch the pavement again. I watched other cars leave the lot, their taillights shrinking into the horizon, while I whispered a silent prayer deep within my engine: *Please, someone choose me. I promise, I am fun to drive.*

That prayer was answered by a lanky high-school junior named Art. My price, a fraction of the Corvette's, matched his thin wallet. Neither of us knew it then, but the next six years would carry us through a whirlwind of teenage adventures—dances, band practices, carnivals, football games, and late-night drives stitched into a grand anthology of youthful dreams.

At first, I was merely a means of transportation. Each morning, precisely at 7:15, I rumbled to the Rexall Drug Store, where Art met the iceman and prepared the soda fountain for opening. After school, I carried him back to work until his assigned chores were complete. Yet soon, I was swept into the vibrancy of high school life.

Because Art was the drum major of the "Owl" marching band, my trunk transformed into a traveling orchestra pit, packed with drums, horns, and uniforms. I lived for the evenings when we carried majorettes to carnival parades, or when we raced the fading sun to football games, the roar of the crowds echoing in my windows as they cheered for the blue and white of the Westminster Owls.

After-game dances brought more delight—teenagers swaying to the latest hit records, boys nervously asking girls for a dance, and at night's end, I ferried couples home under the quiet watch of the stars. Later, when Art became Key Club Lieutenant Governor, I carried him across the highways of Maryland and Virginia, meeting scores of young leaders brimming with energy and ambition.

Saturday nights were my favorite. That was when Art picked up his date. My black leather bucket seats glowed with anticipation, and my newly installed FM tuner filled the cabin with the crisp, static-free sounds of the era. I became the chariot to their world of pep rallies, dances, movies, parties, and even rustic hootenannies where guitars strummed into the night.

One girl, her smile radiant and infectious, became a frequent passenger. Together, we braved winding country roads and slick October snow. Just as suddenly as the snowfall came, she disappeared. Later, she returned briefly—for *Doctor Zhivago* and *West Side Story*—but soon faded again, leaving behind only the haunting strains of "Somewhere" and "Laura's Theme," melodies that clung to my memory like ghosts.

Then came another, her sparkling blue eyes framed by the poise of a senior who wore the crown of Football Formal Queen. With her, nights shone brighter. At the Lions Club Fashion Formal, they dazzled the crowd in elegant attire. Their adventures filled chapters worth retelling: front-row balcony seats at the Baltimore premiere of *The Sound of Music*, searching in vain for a restaurant serving breakfast at 2 a.m., a graduation party, even a near-marooning during a blizzard. Yet distance proved stronger than affection. When a letter arrived, announcing she had chosen another, I braced myself for the ache of losing yet another treasured passenger.

September 1965 ushered in a new chapter: College Park. Through pounding rain, I carried Art to the University of Maryland, my trunk crammed with the clutter of dorm life and my back seat piled with freshly pressed clothes. College brought more than lectures—it brought friendships, intramural sports, and Friday mixers alive with local bands echoing the music of the Beatles and the Rolling Stones.

It was there that a tall, lively brunette nursing student slid into my passenger seat. Under the glow of Washington's monuments, the city lights reflected in her eyes. She laughed easily, and for a time, her warmth comforted Art, especially after the death of his grandmother. But as the winter thawed, so too did their connection, and one day she was gone.

Next came Baltimore, where the grind of pharmacy education replaced youthful ease. My days carried Art to The Johns Hopkins Hospital, where he balanced evening shifts with academic demands. I bore witness to the city's chaos— the hum of traffic, the clang of construction, even the tense, smoke-filled days of the 1968 riots when the emergency rooms overflowed with the injured. In those years, the small-town boy from Carroll County began to grow into a man.

And then, in 1968, everything changed. A green-eyed brunette from Towson State entered the picture. Unlike the others, her presence brought quiet certainty. Their shared roots and deepening affection blossomed into a love that eclipsed all before it.

But time had worn on me. My springs sagged, my shocks groaned, and one cold December night, after a fraternity Christmas party, I surrendered. I was traded away for a sleek blue-and-white Buick.

From the used car underground, I heard whispers of their wedding and honeymoon. Though I was no longer there, the memories I carried—the laughter, the heartbreak, the milestones of seven unforgettable years—remain etched into my steel frame. If such a place exists, I have earned my place in the Used Car Hall of Fame.

FIRST KISS

"The sound of a kiss is not so loud as a cannon, but its echo lasts a great deal longer."
— Oliver Wendell Holmes, American Jurist

Summertime, a canvas of lazy, sun-drenched days,
Escape from weekly exams and crowded hallways.
Backyard barbecues, a prelude to midway's call,
Promising carnival fun and laughter for all.

Teenagers gather each night beneath the fading sun,
Hypnotized by multi-colored lights, searching for fun.
Among the tents, "carny" games provide the play,
As the scent of crab cakes and fries fill the midway.

Midweek parades attract crowds filled with delight,
As high school bands march proudly, a spectacular sight.
Brass trumpets blare Sousa marches filling the night air.
Majorettes and drummers strut with a confident flair.

After each parade, carnival lights call once more,
Enticing teenagers to the bandstand's dance floor.
Couples sway to rock 'n' roll music, lost in each other's gaze.
Dancing to sixties melodies, hypnotized in the music's haze.

Then one parade night, she appeared in twilight's glow,
Her whimsical smile mirroring the sunset's light show.
Drawn by the scent of her perfume, we stayed out late,
The majorette and I rode each ride on our first date.

Each fun-filled evening together struck a positive note,
With every dance and nickel pitched, a hopeful heart spoke.
A quiet thought, or whisper, evoked a silent, hopeful prayer.
Like the Ferris wheel's slow turn, we cherish moments we share.

A gentle summer breeze whispered the time was right,
Yet second thoughts cast doubt; could this be the night?
With her head on my shoulder, I felt a tender sway.
Her touch emboldened me; I hadn't kissed a girl until today.

The August moon urged us closer in a shared embrace.
Her eyes sparkled like stars as their reflection danced on her face.
A magical moment as trembling arms surrounded my miss,
Her tender touch inspired our memorable first kiss.

The Gift

"Every gift is a reflection of the giver's thoughts and feelings."
— Anonymous

Gifts mark moments and etch memories. They can be tangible, like the small, shimmering circle pin that once carried the weight of my sixteen-year-old heart, or intangible, etched into our very being, shaping how we learn to love and connect. Both kinds of gifts leave an imprint that time cannot erase.

It was 1963, a year alive with change. Jimmy Gilmer and the Fireballs' *Sugar Shack* drifted through radios across America, while the Beatles' first U.S. release, *She Loves You,* was climbing the charts. Amidst that soundtrack of shifting times, a smile in junior English class caught my attention—bright, effortless, and magnetic. I was drawn in instantly. Carrying her books became my excuse to linger near her, each chance encounter charged with a quiet thrill. When I finally gathered the courage to ask her out, her simple "yes" felt like the start of everything.

Those autumn weeks were a whirlwind—Friday night football games under glowing stadium lights, school dances where the music seemed to play only for us, the electric brush of her hand against mine, the comfort of her head resting on my shoulder. In those fleeting moments, I discovered my first true intangible gift: the awakening of mutual attraction, the dizzying realization of being seen, wanted, and cherished by someone beyond family.

As the leaves fell and December neared, Christmas began to take on a new meaning. It was no longer just the sparkle of ornaments or the excitement of wrapped boxes beneath the tree. It was her, seated at the piano, fingers dancing across the keys as carols filled the room. Her music carried a depth that made the Christmas story feel alive, radiant with grace. In that season, the lure of material gifts faded into the background, replaced by a deeper understanding: Christmas was a reminder of God's gift of peace, of love freely given. This became the second intangible gift—a spiritual awakening that stirred something lasting within me.

Yet intangible gifts often yearn for something tangible to hold them. I wanted to give her a token that matched the feeling she had awakened in me. My meager wages from the Rexall Drug Store narrowed my choices, but after days of searching, I found it—a delicate circle pin, its sparkle reminding me of the light in her eyes. It was a stretch for my budget, but it felt right, as though it belonged to her from the beginning.

The anticipation sat heavy in my stomach when the day came. The small wrapped box pressed against the inside of my pocket like a heartbeat. Would she understand? Would she see in it what I hoped to say but could not yet put into words?

Her smile when she arrived quieted every doubt. When she unwrapped the pin, her eyes shone with delight, and I felt my world steady. Then, to my surprise, she reached into her purse and handed me a small box of her own—a gift she had chosen with the same thought and care.

The next day, we wore our gifts to school, a silent pledge of affection for all to see. That moment was more than just youthful romance; it was the first time I felt loved and cherished by someone beyond the circle of family. That Christmas etched a belief deep within me—that love is not only the strongest force on earth but also a divine gift, eternal in its reach.

Our gifts became symbols of more than just a holiday. They captured the fragile beauty of young love, the joy of discovery, and the true spirit of Christmas itself. Just as the wise men once brought their gifts to the Christ child, ours too were offerings, humble yet filled with love.

And then, without warning, it ended. Weeks later, she was gone, leaving behind a silence I could not comprehend. I tried to bridge the distance—another date on New Year's Eve, afternoons at the movies, a performance of *West Side Story*, even a Baltimore Colts football game—but the spark had slipped away. The laughter, the whispered conversations beneath the stars, the sense of unspoken understanding—they all faded like smoke.

Yet the memories have never left me. I still recall the long drives through farmland slowly giving way to suburbs, the radiant curve of her smile, the gentle way her hand would find mine. And always, the pin—a small, glittering reminder of those intangible gifts we gave each other.

The joy of that first love and the ache of its sudden ending prepared me for the deeper, steadier love I would one day find. The hurt and the memory of the pin remain, not as regrets, but as reminders: of a love that was, and a love that was not meant to last.

OCTOBER MOON

"It is a beautiful and delightful sight to behold the body of the moon."
— *Galileo Galilei, Italian mathematician, physicist, philosopher, and astronomer*

Late summer evenings hear the cricket's muted serenade.
August nights expose glowing fireflies marching in a parade.
Once green in June, the farmer's fields now gleam in gold.
Shorter days murmur of summer's passing, as warmth turns cold.

September's first cool breeze invites emerald leaves to take flight.
Auburn skies herald autumn beneath the October moon's light.
A perfect amber sphere ascends after dusk, along the skyline,
Climbing through the shadows, deliberating, crafting autumn's design.

Its glow mingles with the stars that watch the world below.
Illuminating fields once teeming with corn, awaiting winter's snow.
Apple-laden branches promise tasty dumplings and yummy pies,
As the October moon rises high, hiding secrets in the skies.

The silent October moon witnesses as summer's memories fade.
Keeping secret thoughts of lingering warmer days, no longer displayed.
Emerging cooler days stifle prospects of a late-season encore.
While hot spiced cider, with gingerbread, warms each evening's lure.

Autumn unfolds with football cheers and bands in Halloween parades.
As an early frost sets the stage for cozy hayrides and love unafraid.
Wagon wheels adoring whispers on a bumpy wooded track,
Beneath arching branches, the crunch of leaves escorts each wheel's clack.

Crimson clouds dance among treetops as daylight disappears too soon.
As the moon peaks from cottony clouds like a child's lost balloon.
The tawny sphere listens to couples' dreams born on a starlit path.
As arms linked and hands entwine, they shelter from the breeze's nippy bath.

The October moon smiles softly, bearing witness to a first embrace,
Foretelling whispered secrets and adventures time won't erase.

Vibrant autumn hues paint a canvas where young dreams reside,
An autumn chill recedes, warmed by hearts that beat side by side.

Silently, without warning, lifetime memories take shape,
Crafted by nature's gentle hand, leaving in our hearts a landscape.
October wanes to a crescent moon, a signal of November's chill,
While warmer days retreat, like fields beneath the harvest still.

Gray skies filled with honking geese beneath the north wind's sharp cry,
Enduring cold rains and inevitable snow, we watch the days drift by.
Winter's cold will challenge the inspiration of autumn's haunting tune,
But seasons pass, memories endure, fashioned under the October moon.

Faith: The Mandatory Ingredient of Life

Foundation of Faith

"Faith never knows where it is being led, but it loves and knows the One who is leading."
— Oswald Chambers, Scottish Evangelist

The book of Hebrews describes faith as *"the confident assurance that something we want is going to happen. It is the certainty that what we hope is waiting for us, even though we cannot see it up ahead. By believing in God, we know that the world, the stars, and all things were made by God from things that can't be seen."*

This definition resonates deeply with my own faith journey. My belief has been shaped through personal experiences, biblical truth, and the quiet guidance of the Holy Spirit.

Beyond the teaching I received at home, some of my earliest encounters with faith began at St. Paul's, my home church. Patient and devoted Sunday School teachers introduced me to the love of Christ, planting the first seeds of spiritual growth. Those early lessons gave me a foundation that would support me through life's unfolding seasons.

As I grew older, the meaning of Christmas began to take on greater depth. What once seemed to be a festive holiday became a profound reminder of God's gift to the world. Each passing year revealed new layers of understanding—lessons about sacrifice, hope, and renewal—enriching the way I experienced faith and celebrated the season.

A turning point in my journey came when I met Vickie, my life partner. She shared her deep and steady faith, encouraging me to explore new ways of seeing God's presence in my life. Together, we discovered how faith could guide not only individuals but also a marriage built on trust and prayer.

My path gained further meaning through service as a lay speaker at Calvary United Methodist Church. In the early 1990s, encouraged by my pastor, I began leading laity Sundays. Preparing a Sunday morning message became one of my most powerful teachers. Each message demanded study, reflection, and honest self-examination. In wrestling with Scripture and considering how to share it, I found myself drawn ever closer to God.

The Bible, with its collection of stories, parables, and teachings, continues to be a vital framework for understanding how God interacts with humanity. Its narratives show us faith in action—how ordinary people encountered extraordinary moments of God's presence. Through these accounts, we see how faith is both lived and tested, and how it becomes the foundation for our relationship with God.

One of the most profound examples is found in the story of Lazarus in John 11.

- **Jesus is the Resurrection and the Life:** This truth forms the core of Christian belief. The raising of Lazarus was not only a miracle but also a revelation of Jesus' authority over life and death. It foreshadowed His own resurrection and revealed His divine identity to Mary, Martha, and all who were present. The moment invited them—and invites us—to declare our faith in Him. Even now, two thousand years later, the scene at Bethany compels us to renew our trust in the promise of resurrection. When Jesus commanded the stone to be rolled away and called Lazarus to come forth, He was extending the same invitation to each of us: to step out of whatever binds us, to leave behind the darkness of despair, and to walk into the light of His love—a love stronger than the grave itself.

- **The Supreme Power of God:** The miracle at Bethany was not only about Lazarus but about God's limitless authority. The Old Testament tells of God's power through stories of deliverance and creation, but here a new chapter unfolded. Just as David sang of God's strength in the Psalms, Jesus demonstrated that this same power was at work in Him. Such power is not distant—it is available to us through faith in Christ. To embrace it fully, however, requires surrender: a willingness to lay down our illusion of control and place our trust in God's timing and plan. When we do, we discover peace and fulfillment beyond anything the world can offer.

- **The Glory of God is in All Things:** In church, we often speak of "God's glory," but what does it truly mean? His glory is revealed in creation—the majesty of mountains, the stillness of forests, the birth of a child, and the quiet strength of love shared between people. It appears in everyday moments, often overlooked: a soul finding redemption, a spirit renewed, a flower blooming in season. These glimpses remind us that God is not distant but deeply invested in our lives. Just as a grandchild instinctively reaches for the guiding hand of a grandparent, we are invited to reach for God's hand and recognize His role as the source of all goodness.

In John 11, God's glory is fully unveiled. Through Christ, God declares: *"This is who I am. This is my Son with all authority. I will rescue you from death. My love will guide you. I will be with you no matter what you face."* In this revelation, God offers us the freedom to choose—to either embrace His glory or turn away. His love is constant, but His greatest gift is allowing us to respond freely to His call.

The life and witness of Dietrich Bonhoeffer, a twentieth-century pastor and theologian who suffered under Nazi rule, also shed light on the nature of faith and grace. Bonhoeffer warned against what he called "cheap grace"—grace that costs us nothing, requires no transformation, and avoids the cross. In contrast, he spoke of "costly grace"—a grace rooted in the gospel, marked by sacrifice, and demanding genuine discipleship. It is a grace that requires us to follow Christ, even when it means walking difficult roads. His distinction between the two remains a reminder that authentic faith cannot be passive; it must be lived out with courage and devotion.

Faith, then, is not a static possession but a journey of continual discovery. It asks us to acknowledge Jesus as the way, the truth, and the life. It calls us to rely on God's power and direction, especially when life feels uncertain or overwhelming. As our faith matures, we begin to recognize the subtle ways God works in our lives—through unexpected blessings, quiet nudges of the Spirit, and the strength He provides in moments of weakness.

Looking back on my own journey, I see how these principles have guided me. From Sunday School lessons to lay speaking, from marriage to personal trials, each step has been marked by God's presence. My prayer is that I have lived out these truths as fully as God intends, and that my faith continues to grow deeper in trust, stronger in love, and more steadfast in hope.

The Many Faces of God's Grace

"Grace comes into the soul, as the morning sun into the world; first a dawning; then a light; and at last, the sun in his full and excellent brightness."

— Thomas Adams, American Inventor

Everyone cherishes the love and thoughtfulness behind a well-chosen gift. A gift is more than a simple gesture—it's an expression of care, love, and connection between the giver and the receiver. It carries meaning beyond its physical form, often creating a lasting memory, especially when it comes unexpectedly.

We receive gifts from family, friends, and loved ones on birthdays, holidays, and moments of celebration. Some gifts are tangible—something we can hold and see—while others are unseen, yet deeply felt. These intangible gifts often leave the greatest impact on our hearts. The perfect gift, however, is one given freely—without expectation, without condition, and without measure. It endures, renews, and uplifts. Though it may seem almost unimaginable that such a gift could exist, there is one that meets all these qualities: the eternal and boundless gift of God's Grace.

Mentioned more than 170 times throughout Scripture—from Genesis to Revelation—grace is described as God's unearned favor, freely poured out on all who believe. It is an ever-flowing stream of love, mercy, and divine strength that sustains us through every season of life.

In 2 Peter 1:3, we are reminded that God's grace provides "everything we need for life and godliness." This includes not only the material blessings that meet our daily needs but also the spiritual strength to face life's challenges, the wisdom to make righteous choices, and the hope that anchors us in the promise of eternal life. Salvation, the most precious of all gifts, is extended to every heart willing to accept the hand of Christ—a hand offered not as a response to our deeds but as a reflection of God's generous and loving nature.

God's grace is present in countless ways, shaping our lives and guiding our steps:

- **In our relationships:** Every person we meet—family, friends, colleagues, and even strangers—can be a vessel of God's grace. Through their love, encouragement, and presence, we experience glimpses of His care and compassion.
- **In our talents and abilities:** The unique gifts and skills we possess are no accident. They are divine blessings, meant to bring glory to God and serve others with purpose and joy.
- **In answered prayers:** Whether we cry out for direction, healing, or comfort, God listens. His responses may not always align with our expectations, yet they often reveal a wisdom beyond our understanding—reminding us that His grace works in ways both seen and unseen.
- **In the promise of salvation:** The greatest expression of grace is found in the gift of salvation through Jesus Christ. Through His sacrifice, we are reconciled with God, given new life, and assured of eternal hope.

Recognizing and embracing this grace requires more than acknowledgment—it calls for a life transformed by gratitude

and love. To truly live in the light of God's grace, we are invited to:
- **Serve others:** Extend compassion, kindness, and understanding to those in need, mirroring the selfless love that God shows to us each day.
- **Live in gratitude:** Cultivate a thankful heart that recognizes every blessing as a sign of God's presence, inspiring us to live with purpose and humility.
- **Share our faith:** Speak of God's goodness and love, so that others may also experience the joy and renewal found in His grace.

When we open our hearts to grace, it reshapes us from within. It awakens compassion, strengthens our faith, and equips us to serve others with deeper sincerity.

As I reflect on my own journey, I often wonder whether my actions truly align with God's expectations—whether my service reflects His will. Yet even amid moments of doubt, I see evidence of transformation in my life, a change deeply rooted in the love and support of those God has placed around me.

Some individuals from my past have quietly faded from view, yet their influence lingers in the lessons they left behind. Others remain steadfast presences in my heart—my parents, whose steadfast guidance molded my character; my in-laws, whose warmth and acceptance made me feel at home; and Vickie, my partner in every sense, whose insight and encouragement continue to inspire my walk of faith.

One of Vickie's favorite songs carries a line that captures this truth perfectly: *"Someone had a hand in it long before we ever knew."* These words remind me that God's grace often works behind the scenes—through people, moments, and choices we may not fully understand until later. His hand has been guiding, shaping, and preparing us for His purpose long before we recognized it.

In conclusion, God's grace is an inexhaustible well of strength, hope, and joy. When we recognize its presence, nurture a heart of gratitude, and strive to live in alignment with its principles, we experience a profound transformation—one that illuminates our path and draws us closer to the heart of God. Through every blessing, challenge, and moment of growth, we come to see the many faces of His grace—ever present, ever faithful, and ever renewing.

Shadows and Sunlight

"I am the light of the world. Whoever follows me will never walk in darkness but will have the light of life."

— John 8:12

Margaret Thatcher once wisely cautioned, "Standing in the middle of the road is very dangerous; you get knocked down by traffic from both directions." This truth vividly portrays the peril of indecision—the state of those often called "fence sitters." Such individuals hesitate to take a stand, caught between two opposing paths, never fully at ease in either the shadows or the sunlight.

From the very beginning of creation, light and darkness were set in contrast—two fundamental forces shaping existence. This duality echoes through every aspect of life: love and hate, joy and sorrow, good and evil. These pairs, while sometimes balancing one another, often symbolize the opposing powers constantly at work within the human heart.

God, in His divine wisdom, created both light and darkness and declared that "the light was good." He separated the day from the night, each with its own purpose. The presence of shadows, though sometimes unsettling, plays a vital role in creation. Darkness is part of life's rhythm—necessary for rest, reflection, and growth. Even in its stillness, darkness holds meaning. Artists use shadows to give their work dimension; nature uses night to restore its strength. The deep ebony of the night sky frames the brilliance of the stars, reminding us that beauty is often most visible against contrast.

Children instinctively recognize the playfulness within darkness—turning twilight's long shadows into allies during games of hide and seek. Yet, human nature leans toward the light. We are drawn to warmth, clarity, and understanding. We seek out the sun, chase enlightenment, and long to live in truth's glow.

History, too, bears witness to the power of light. At dawn over Fort McHenry during the War of 1812, the morning rays revealed the American flag still waving, a vision that moved Francis Scott Key to write the words of *The Star-Spangled Banner*. That moment—light overcoming darkness—became a lasting symbol of hope and endurance.

But the pursuit of light extends far beyond the physical. It reaches into the soul's deepest chambers, where spiritual darkness can take root. This darkness, born of sin and estrangement from God, is the most dangerous of all. The Bible recounts the dramatic transformation of Saul, a man once consumed by hatred for Christians. Through divine intervention, he became Paul—the tireless apostle who carried God's light to the world. His life stands as living proof that no one is beyond redemption, and that divine light can pierce even the thickest shadows of sin.

Today, our world remains veiled in many layers of spiritual darkness. Temptations abound. Power, greed, and worldly pleasure promise fulfillment but deliver emptiness. Without faith, loss and disappointment can consume us. The death of a loved one, the unraveling of a relationship, or a sudden life challenge can plunge us into despair if our hearts are not anchored in Christ.

To step out of the shadows and walk in the light, we must take intentional steps of faith:

1. Acknowledge our limitations.

Recognizing our human frailty is the first act of humility. We are not self-sufficient. God knows every pressure and sorrow we face, for Jesus Himself walked this earth. When we admit our need for divine help, He stands ready to guide and strengthen us.

2. Confess our sins.

Spiritual renewal begins with honesty. In his letter to the Galatians, Paul urges believers to break free from legalistic rituals and worldly distractions. He reminds us that sincere confession invites Christ's forgiveness and grace. True repentance is not merely an admission of wrongs—it is a turning point where the soul chooses restoration over rebellion.

3. Ask for God's help.

Prayer is not a ritual; it is a lifeline. Regular, heartfelt communion with God strengthens our faith and brings clarity amid confusion. Through prayer, we seek not only answers but also peace, courage, and purpose. In moments of hardship, this connection becomes a steady light that reminds us we are never alone.

4. Love unconditionally.

To walk in the light is to love as Christ loved—without condition or hesitation. We are called to extend kindness and compassion to every soul we encounter. This love is not abstract; it must be visible in our actions, our words, and our willingness to forgive. When we love sincerely, we reflect the very heart of God to a world in need of warmth.

The great evangelist Billy Graham observed that any attempt to organize life apart from God leads only to frustration and despair. Without divine guidance, humanity's self-worship ends in emptiness, for no earthly achievement can satisfy the soul's deepest longing.

Faith, therefore, demands more than passive belief—it requires courage and commitment. It calls us to step off the fence of indecision and walk boldly into Christ's radiant light. Like the Samaritan woman at the well, once touched by the "living water," we must share the good news with others, becoming beacons of hope in a darkened world.

God places each of us on a lampstand, not to hide our faith, but to let it shine. The decision is ours: remain cloaked in the shadows of doubt, or embrace the transforming brilliance of Christ's light.

The invitation stands open. Step down from the fence. Let Christ lead you from uncertainty into purpose, from darkness into life.

Christmas Is

"Christmas is the day that holds all time together."
— Alexander Smith, Scottish Poet

Each year, we find ourselves drawn once more to rediscover the meaning of Christmas.

For children, it is a treasure hunt through mountains of wrapped packages, shimmering tinsel, and the twinkle of multi-colored lights—all watched over by a jolly man with a white beard and crimson suit.

For adolescents, the season carries a growing understanding—each retelling of the nativity revealing deeper truths about faith, sacrifice, and joy.

For adults, it is a pilgrimage of memory. They stand before the manger, drawing upon cherished traditions and heartfelt recollections, reflecting on the miracle that changed the world.

Rediscovering Christmas invites us to explore its many dimensions—a celebration rich with history, steeped in tradition, and alive with promise for the future. Like Ebenezer Scrooge, who faced his own neglect of the season's spirit, we too are called to pause and examine our hearts, to seek the sacred essence beneath the glitter and noise.

Perhaps our own Christmas memories—woven with faith, family, and gratitude—form a personal answer to the timeless question: *What is Christmas?* It is a definition shaped by beloved customs, comforting aromas, familiar melodies, and, above all, the Christ Child at the center of it all.

My own Christmas is rooted in childhood innocence, a season overflowing with anticipation.

The countdown began each year on December 26. My sisters and I would carefully chart the long march of 365 days until the next celebration. Though our early enthusiasm often faded by midyear, it was reignited every autumn when the *Sears Roebuck* catalog arrived — our cherished "Wish Book."

We'd flip straight to the toy section, ignoring the pages of socks and sweaters, our eyes scanning every bright image and new gadget. That two-inch-thick catalog, with Santa smiling on its glossy cover, became our portal to dreams. Its pages soon grew soft and wrinkled from our eager fingers as we built our wish lists and imagined the wonders to come.

Christmas morning was the culmination of all that waiting — a day when wishes seemed to come alive.

Stockings brimmed with simple treasures. One of my greatest joys was discovering the *Life Saver® Book* — a small folder filled with rolls of candy that replaced the cookies and *Coca-Cola®* we'd left for Santa the night before. Beneath the tree, the gifts from the jovial elf were magical: a new baseball bat and ball, a gleaming football helmet, or — on one unforgettable morning — a *Schwinn* bicycle for each of us.

Technology was not yet part of Christmas. The most advanced gift was a new record player, capable of playing at 33 ⅓, 45, and 78 RPM — an innovation that filled our home with music and joy.

Yet beyond the gifts, the heart of Christmas beat strongest in our family gatherings and festive meals.

Brunch with our extended family filled the house with warmth. The air carried the scent of hot chocolate, eagerly awaited by eight cousins, and the savory aroma of oyster stew—lovingly prepared by my grandfather for the seafood lovers among us. Platters of sweet rolls, delicate pastries, and bursts of laughter filled the table.

The celebration continued into dinner. The kitchen was alive with the fragrance of mincemeat, cinnamon, and Christmas pudding. Our feast featured steak and French fries, homemade cranberry relish, and the crown jewel—Grammie Riley's famous butterscotch pie.

No meal was complete without my grandmother's *sand tarts*: thin, buttery cookies baked to golden perfection. Each was decorated with care, though my favorite were the ones dusted with cinnamon sugar.

The sights and sounds of Christmas deepened the season's spirituality.

Outside, a towering tree adorned with glowing lights could be seen from a mile away. Around town, cheerful Santas greeted shoppers, poinsettias brightened windowsills, nutcrackers stood guard, and candles flickered gently against frosted glass.

Inside our home, the air carried the fresh scent of pine from the wreaths my mother lovingly crafted, and the evergreen tree stood tall, dressed with ornaments passed down through generations. But it was the Nativity scene that completed the picture—our most sacred decoration, a humble reminder of divine love entering the world.

Music filled every corner of our celebration.

The first carol I learned, "Away in a Manger," began a lifelong love of Christmas hymns. As the years passed, that love matured through caroling with neighbors, high school concerts, and listening to the timeless voices of Crosby, Como, Cole, Clooney, and Page. The majestic tones of the pipe organ swelled through church walls, carrying the divine message of hope and redemption.

Even the wistful notes of "I'll Be Home for Christmas" spoke to the heart, echoing the longing of a college student heading home after final exams, eager to return to the warmth of family and faith.

In town, Christmas brought a chorus of sounds—the steady ringing of the Salvation Army bell, the clink of coins in red kettles, and the delighted laughter of children spotting Santa on the street. Each sound carried a message of generosity and love.

On Christmas Eve, church bells filled the air while I stood behind the counter at the local drugstore, wrapping box after box of *Russell Stover* chocolates. Strangers exchanged greetings with the warmth of old friends, and for a brief moment, the entire community seemed united in goodwill.

But the most profound sound was silence.

As we stepped out from the candlelight service, the world seemed to hold its breath. The night sky shimmered with stars—unchanged since the shepherds first looked upon them in Bethlehem. In that quiet stillness, faith settled into our hearts, reminding us of the miracle of God's love made flesh in the Christ Child.

The Christ Child entered a world of turmoil, much like our own. Yet in the hills of Judea, angels proclaimed news of great joy—a Savior born for all people. The shepherds received the message first, humble witnesses to a moment that would change eternity. Through their story, we too are invited to kneel before the manger and discover the peace that only faith can bring.

To walk the road to Bethlehem is to choose a path of renewal—a journey toward deeper faith and steadfast love. That commitment means:

- Extending the joy and hope of Christmas through kindness, recognizing the divine spark within every soul.
- Reflecting on the magnitude of that first Christmas, crafted by God's design, and His boundless love for humanity.
- Keeping Mary, Joseph, and the Christ Child at the heart of every celebration.
- Rekindling our faith each year, allowing the light of Christmas to shine through our lives.

When we sing of "peace on earth" and "joy to the world," those words must echo through our actions. A Christmas built solely on material treasures risks obscuring the season's true meaning. Though the feasts, decorations, and carols bring beauty, they are but reflections of a greater light—the brilliance of the Christmas star guiding us toward hope, mercy, and the everlasting love of Christ.

Christmas is a living symphony—an anthem of joy expressed in countless ways.

It is the promise carried in a newborn's cry, the boundless possibility of a life entrusted to faith, the dawning of a new and glorious morning.

It is the love that entered the world in a humble stable, the love that still transforms hearts today.

Each year, as our memories drift softly through time, they remind us of the traditions handed down with care and the unshakable faith that sustains them.

What is Christmas?

It is the sum of all these moments—faith remembered, love renewed, and the presence of God made real through the birth of His Son.

Are We Listening?

"Do not merely listen to the word and so deceive yourselves. Do what it says."
— James 1:22

In the quiet moments, amidst the busyness and constant motion of our lives, a profound question echoes:

Are we truly listening to God?

The inspired words of the New Testament have deeply shaped my journey as a lay speaker. I treasure the privilege of sharing these sacred stories and parables, much like the hymn declares, *"I Love to Tell the Story."* Within these passages lie the core truths of a living faith: the immeasurable love of God, the central role of Jesus Christ, and our shared calling to proclaim His word. My hope is that my reflections encourage others to look inward, examine their faith, and strengthen their service to Christ.

But before we can speak His message with conviction, we must first learn to listen—truly and wholeheartedly.

Our natural response might be, *"Of course, we listen!"* Yet if we are honest, the evidence often reveals otherwise. Many of us are quick to prepare a response before the other person has even finished speaking. Our minds run ahead of the words, leaving little room for genuine understanding. Sometimes we interrupt, assuming we already know what's coming, eager to offer our opinion before truly hearing the heart of the message.

Too often, our prayer life reflects this same impatience. We bring our petitions before God, pour out our concerns, and then rush ahead — filling the silence instead of resting in it. We may even find ourselves anticipating or dictating the answer we expect, rather than waiting with an open spirit for God's reply.

Yet God does respond — just not always in the way or at the pace we expect. Listening, therefore, becomes a sacred act, an essential part of our relationship with Him. In the stillness, if we dare to pause and quiet our hearts, we may be surprised by what He gently speaks into our souls.

But how can we truly hear God's voice if we doubt His love?

Dr. Judith Jones, Professor of Religion at Wartburg College, offers this reassuring truth: *"If we ever should question whether God genuinely loves us, the gift and witness of the Holy Spirit confirms that we are God's beloved. God's love is a truth more basic and dependable than the ground we walk on and the air we breathe."*

When we rest in this unwavering love, our hearts open more freely. We begin to trust His voice, even when it calls us to growth, change, or surrender. Confidence in God's love is the firm foundation upon which genuine listening is built.

Nowhere is this divine love more powerfully revealed than in the Easter season. Easter is more than a celebration of spring's return; it is a living testimony to God's infinite grace. The empty tomb stands as a bold declaration that love conquers death, urging us to listen more deeply, to seek understanding, and to share the life-changing hope of the resurrection with others.

This holy season calls us to mirror that love — to nurture compassion, to place Jesus firmly at the center of our lives, and to allow His message to shape our actions.

To do so, we must guard against the noise and distractions of the world—those subtle temptations that pull our attention away from Christ. Making Jesus our anchor means relinquishing our need for control and trusting His guidance completely.

When our faith is strong, it becomes our compass, realigning us with God's will even when our human nature tempts us to steer our own course. In surrendering, we invite His transformative love to work through us—renewing our hearts, our homes, and our communities with the hope and joy of Easter.

My own journey as a lay speaker has been a continual lesson in the discipline of listening. Through study, prayer, and reflection, I've discovered that engaging deeply with Scripture allows me not only to hear God's word but to share it more meaningfully with others.

Just as the disciples used their unique gifts to spread the Gospel across the world, we too are called to share our testimonies—grounded in Scripture and shaped by devotion, discipleship, and love. When we speak from the teachings of Christ, we don't just tell stories—we reveal how faith has touched our own lives and how His truth continues to guide us.

Cultivating true listening requires humility. It calls for silencing the chatter of our thoughts, giving full attention to the speaker, and seeking to understand rather than to respond. It asks us to withhold judgment, to ask gentle questions, and to let compassion guide our hearing.

This discipline extends not only to our conversations with others but also to our communion with God. We practice spiritual listening by carving out moments of silence, meditating on Scripture, and noticing how God may speak through unexpected means—a friend's encouragement, a challenging circumstance, or the quiet prompting of the heart.

As we walk in faith, learning to listen becomes inseparable from our calling to love and to serve. Understanding God's love, centering our lives on Jesus, and sharing His word—all depend on our willingness to listen with patience, expectation, and open hearts.

God may not speak according to our schedule, but when He does, His message is complete. Our role is not to edit or reshape His words to fit our desires but to receive them fully, trusting that His truth will always lead us toward love and service.

Being a good listener is not passive—it is an act of love, a ministry in itself, and it prepares us to share our own story with sincerity and grace.

I hold dear the privilege of telling God's story as I've come to understand it. My ability to listen is still being refined, as is true for us all. But faith strengthens my hearing—it reminds me that His voice always leads toward compassion, forgiveness, and unity.

We can trust that God's message will consistently call us to love our neighbors and to serve faithfully within our communities. And all of this begins with the quiet courage to listen—both to the Word and to one another.

For it is in those still, attentive moments that we discern the whisper of divine love and find the strength to carry His story into the world.

So when we hear—are we truly listening?

To tell His story well, we must first listen deeply.

Go Find Jesus

"You are looking for Jesus the Nazarene, who was crucified. He has risen!"
— Mark 16:6

The Gospels of Matthew, Mark, Luke, and John reveal the Easter story — a message that has echoed through centuries and continues to stir the hearts of believers today. It carries a truth as simple as it is profound: Christ is risen! This declaration is not a distant historical record or a seasonal tradition we revisit each spring. It is a living, urgent call that speaks directly to each of us, reminding us that the resurrection is not merely an event — it is an invitation to hope.

In our modern age, we often approach faith with an analytical lens, striving to dissect the miraculous and rationalize the mystery. Yet the empty tomb resists such examination. It stands as a powerful emblem of triumph — Christ's victory over death itself. This sacred moment urges us to pause and reflect on the mysteries of life and mortality, inviting us to embrace the hope that extends beyond the grave. Though we may attempt to reason through it, Easter ultimately transcends explanation. The message remains gloriously simple: Jesus Christ was raised from the dead, and through His sacrifice, redemption was secured for all humanity.

The narrative of Holy Week is one of divine orchestration — an unfolding plan that established the authority of the Son of Man. From the jubilant procession of Palm Sunday to the dark betrayal in Gethsemane, from the agony of Good Friday's cross to the sorrow of those who watched Him breathe His last—each moment was sacred, intentional, and full of meaning. Then came the dawn of the third day: the stone rolled away, the tomb found empty, and the world forever changed by the risen Lord.

Like Mary Magdalene and the other women who approached the tomb at sunrise, we too may find ourselves bewildered by the sight of emptiness where we expected finality. The stone no longer sealed the grave; only the burial linens remained. Confusion gave way to awe as the angel declared, "He is not here; He has risen." Even then, the reality was almost too wonderful to grasp.

But the empty tomb was never meant to be a puzzle—it was a summons. A divine directive echoing through the ages: "Go find my Son." This is the very heart of Easter. To find Jesus is to find life eternal, to awaken to grace, and to begin a relationship with the living God. Easter offers hope that overcomes despair, love that shatters hatred, forgiveness that restores the broken, and the promise of a radiant life beyond this one. When we lose sight of these truths, we complicate what was meant to be simple. The empty tomb is pure grace—God's love laid bare for all to see. As Billy Graham once reminded us, Jesus loved sinners, even those who did not deserve it. That is grace—unearned, undeserved, but freely given.

Though the world today looks vastly different from the land of Galilee two millennia ago, God's longing for communion with His children has not changed. Imagine, for a moment, a message appearing on your phone or scribbled on a note: "Go find Jesus." How would you respond? Would you dismiss it as a coincidence or pause to wonder what it meant? The Easter message reminds us that God's call isn't confined to a single Sunday. Every day, He invites us to draw near, to seek His Son with open hearts.

But where do we begin this sacred search? The Gospels offer clues. Jesus dwells where pain and need are present. He whispers in the hearts of the weary and embraces those who mourn. He stands beside the sick, the lonely, and the forgotten. In *Matthew 11:28*, He offers this invitation: "Come to me, all who are weary and burdened, and I will give you rest." We can glimpse His presence in a mother's joy, a stranger's kindness, an act of quiet service, or a moment of undeserved forgiveness. Wherever love, mercy, and compassion flourish—there you will find Him. Jesus is wherever He is needed most.

Still, we often forget that we are not meant to search alone. Jesus is not a distant figure to be discovered through effort; He is near—closer than our breath, waiting for us to call His name. Through every hardship and question, He stands ready to walk beside us. The choice is ours: to remain in the emptiness of a life untouched by His grace, or to answer the call of the empty tomb and step into His radiant light, overflowing love, and eternal promise.

Dr. Norman Vincent Peale once observed, "Easter experiences have been happening ever since the first Easter. They happen every day. They can happen to you, and they can happen to me." These experiences may not come as dramatic visions but as quiet moments—a prayer whispered in need, a comforting word from a friend, a peace that arrives unbidden. Each one is an Easter encounter, renewing hearts, lifting spirits, and rekindling faith in those who feel lost or forgotten.

The Easter story is not distant history—it is deeply personal. A divine conversation between you and your Savior. As you turn away from the tomb, let your heart be open to His call: "Go find Jesus." You may be surprised by where—and how—you find Him.

The message of Easter is unwavering: God loves you. Christ died for you and for the sins of the world. He is risen—

and He will come again. The empty tomb stands as a timeless reminder of that truth. Today, the risen Christ waits with open arms, ready to welcome you into His boundless, eternal love.

What Makes Me Tick

PEOPLE + RELATIONSHIPS + SERVICE

"Relationships are based on four principles: respect, understanding, acceptance, and appreciation."
— Mahatma Gandhi, Indian lawyer

People need people. From the dawn of humanity, our interconnectedness has been the foundation of existence. History, in its sweeping timeline—from small nomadic tribes to thriving civilizations—reveals how deeply our survival and growth depend on community.

Fourteen thousand years ago, groups roamed the Middle East in search of food and shelter. Over time, these scattered bands evolved into settlements and then into great civilizations—Mesopotamia, Egypt, India, China, Peru, and Mesoamerica. Despite vast cultural differences, a shared truth united them all: people gathered to meet their essential needs—food, safety, belonging, and emotional support.

We are inherently social beings, not meant to live in isolation. Human interaction is the heartbeat of happiness and fulfillment.

Separation runs contrary to our nature. Living within a community gives individuals a sense of purpose, while their collective contributions strengthen the whole. Service becomes the natural outgrowth of this shared existence—an offering that nourishes both giver and receiver.

As the saying goes, *"Service to others is the rent you pay for your room on earth."* This principle has guided my personal and professional life, shaping the way I see my place in the world.

The earliest lessons in service came from my family. My grandparents instilled in me a duty to uplift the community, and my parents reinforced the responsibility to "give back."

My first job at Rexall Drug Store brought those lessons to life. The owner, a devoted pharmacist, modeled what it truly meant to serve—responding to people's needs not with transactions, but with genuine care. In an age when profit often overshadows purpose, I learned that authentic service begins with listening and sincerity.

That philosophy guided my professional path—from my early work in hospitals to founding Washington Heights Pharmacy. In hospital settings, I saw the life-changing difference that compassion and attentiveness made.

When working directly with patients, I understood that excellence in care required more than skill—it demanded empathy. In my administrative role, I carried the duty of hiring pharmacists and support staff who shared this commitment, ensuring they had the tools, systems, and encouragement needed to serve effectively.

In the community, our work extended beyond prescriptions. We supported patients navigating serious health challenges, providing home infusion services, medical equipment, and personalized education. Each act of service carried weight. Neglecting that duty was not merely a professional lapse—it risked compounding a patient's suffering.

The gratitude expressed by patients and caregivers remains etched in my memory. Their relief, their thanks—these moments reaffirmed the profound impact of showing up with compassion.

Motivated to give back to the community that had supported my business, I joined Kiwanis—a decision that transformed my understanding of service.

What began as local involvement blossomed into a global mission. Through Kiwanis, I saw how collective action changes lives: helping families recover from loss, funding orphanages, providing for basic needs. Beyond borders, I witnessed hope kindled across continents—Kiwanis women in Panama championing education for Indigenous girls; the maternal and neonatal tetanus vaccination campaign in Cambodia saving countless lives; and the delivery of school supplies to children in a remote Nepalese village.

Each experience moved me deeply, revealing the boundless kindness within people and the immense potential for good when we unite with purpose.

Yet the most profound impact wasn't just in what we accomplished—it was in the people I met along the way.

In every country, I encountered individuals whose selflessness inspired me. I still remember the gentle determination of a woman in Belgium serving a warm meal to hungry homeless children, and the joy on a young French girl's face as she danced after enduring multiple surgeries. These moments impressed upon me that true personal growth comes through connection—each encounter shaping our values and expanding our capacity for empathy.

Looking back, I see a mosaic of lives intertwined with mine—classmates, patients, colleagues, mentors, friends, and family—all leaving their imprint on who I've become. To be molded by so many hands is humbling. It reminds me that our identities are not self-made; they are co-authored by every person who walks beside us.

In a world that often celebrates independence above all else, it's easy to forget that our deepest fulfillment is found not in standing alone but in standing together.

We need one another—more than we often care to admit. Those who overlook this truth miss out on the profound joy and meaning born from connection and service.

It is my hope that by sharing my journey, I may encourage others—especially my children and grandchildren—to embrace this truth: that a life grounded in relationships and dedicated to service is a life truly well lived.

Pieces Create a Mosaic

"One should make one's life a mosaic. Let the general design be good, the colors lively, and the material diversified."
— Marthe Bibesco, Romanian-French Writer

Life is a mosaic, meticulously assembled piece by piece. Every step along our journey, every encounter, every triumph, and every trial contributes a unique fragment to this unfolding design. From the monumental milestones to the quiet, easily overlooked moments, each one plays a role in shaping the portrait of who we become. Much like a puzzle, life slowly reveals itself—every new experience adding shape, depth, and meaning to our individual story.

Certain pieces stand out, defining the structure and direction of our lives. These are the pivotal events—marriage, the birth of a child, the loss of a loved one, a career transformation, or the life-altering reality of illness or injury. They are like border pieces, setting boundaries and forming the framework of our existence.

Other fragments are quieter yet equally essential. They include everyday interactions, passing conversations, and fleeting moments of joy or reflection sparked by a song, a piece of art, or the awe of standing before a sunset. Though subtle, they fill in the spaces and bring texture and color to the whole.

Think about the vast number of people we encounter throughout our lifetime—thousands, perhaps millions. Each leaves some imprint, however faint, on our personal mosaic.

Even a brief exchange with a stranger can alter the tone of our day or shift our perspective in unexpected ways. Combined with our natural temperament and choices, these countless experiences merge to form the intricate design of our identity — our values, convictions, and worldview.

Among all these influences, people shape us most profoundly.

Family members, friends, mentors, and colleagues each contribute vital pieces. Our families — especially parents, grandparents, and older siblings — lay the foundation, instilling early lessons and guiding our first understanding of right and wrong. As we grow, mentors such as teachers, community leaders, and members of our faith family reinforce those values while encouraging us to explore our gifts and potential.

Adolescence introduces its own set of defining moments: first jobs, school dances, first loves. Each new experience adds dimension to the evolving portrait of who we are. In adulthood, our circle widens — friends, trusted advisors, coworkers, and neighbors influence our thinking, shape our beliefs, and guide our choices.

Reflecting on my own life mosaic, I see the strong presence of my family. My grandparents taught me the importance of unity and tradition. My parents set high expectations and modeled resilience. My sisters have been unwavering in their support, always reminding me of where I came from. My in-laws introduced me to new dimensions of integrity and honor.

Early employers impressed upon me the value of ethical business — honesty, respect, and service to community. These lessons became guiding lights in my professional journey. Through community engagement, my worldview expanded, bringing me into contact with people from all walks of life. My service as Kiwanis International President was especially formative — traveling the world, meeting remarkable individuals, and forging friendships that endure to this day.

Each connection, from lifelong friends to brief acquaintances, contributed something meaningful. I cherish their influence, acknowledge the moments I've missed, and remain deeply grateful for the imprints they've left on my heart.

Friendships formed in the classroom remain some of the most enduring threads in my life. From kindergarten through college, classmates have been sources of laughter, support, and shared discovery. Time and distance may separate us, but the bonds we built continue to shape me. The memories we created—late-night study sessions, shared victories, and quiet understanding—remind me of the lasting strength of true companionship.

And then there is love—unexpected, transformative, and deeply human. Falling in love cannot be planned, yet it adds a layer of wonder to life that nothing else can. From that love come children and grandchildren—living reflections of grace, joy, and divine design. These relationships are the moments that make heaven smile.

Beyond people, our experiences—both chosen and unforeseen—mold our outlook. I remember a childhood trip to the western national parks, standing before the grandeur of the Grand Tetons and feeling a reverence that words couldn't capture. That moment ignited a lifelong appreciation for nature's majesty. From the vast wilderness of Yellowstone to the snow-capped Alps, each encounter with the natural world whispers of God's handiwork. Even now, the rhythmic hush of ocean waves or the quiet strength of a mountain vista fills me with awe and gratitude. Each passing year, I find myself more deeply moved by creation's beauty and more attuned to the divine presence within it.

Small gestures also leave lasting impressions. I recall one particularly demanding day at the pharmacy—overwhelmed by impatient customers, I was close to exhaustion. A longtime patron, sensing my strain, disappeared briefly and returned with a milkshake. That simple act of kindness transformed my day, reminding me how even the smallest gesture can renew hope and restore balance. These seemingly minor moments, though often overlooked, are essential pieces of our mosaic.

The arts—visual, musical, and spiritual—enrich life's design further. A single painting can move us beyond time and culture. I'll never forget standing before Rembrandt's *Sacrifice of Isaac* in the Hermitage Museum of St. Petersburg, feeling as though God Himself spoke through the artist's brush. Art can quiet the mind, ease fear, and awaken creativity, offering peace and inspiration in equal measure.

Music, too, is a vital companion—soothing the weary, uplifting the heart, and stirring joy in ways words cannot. It sharpens memory, improves rest, and elevates the spirit. For me, it is as essential as breath.

Faith, above all, anchors and gives meaning to the entire design. It connects us to purpose, to one another, and to the divine. Faith instills dignity, hope, and strength; it is the steady rhythm beneath the mosaic's shifting colors. I believe faith and art share a sacred bond—both reveal glimpses of God's grace, reminding us that life itself is a masterpiece in progress.

Still, mysteries remain. Why do some memories echo louder than others? Why do certain people leave indelible marks, while others fade like whispers? Why do some moments flash with the brilliance of lightning, while others pass softly, almost unnoticed?

Perhaps we'll never fully know. Yet, from the first breath to the final heartbeat, every influence—grand or subtle—adds to the intricate portrait of our existence. Each fragment, no matter how small, holds purpose. Together, they form a singular masterpiece—the mosaic of a life lived, loved, and remembered.

People and Travel

"Don't tell me how educated you are, tell me how much you have traveled."
– Mohammed, Religious Leader

The human experience is a mosaic of people, places, lessons, and moments that shape who we become. For me, travel has been the thread that unites these fragments into a living portrait of discovery and understanding. Each journey I take — whether strolling through the narrow, cobblestone lanes of a quiet European village or sharing laughter and stories with locals in a bustling bazaar — deepens my awareness of the world and of myself.

Travel, at its essence, is not measured in miles but in meaning. It's the unplanned conversations that linger in memory, the stillness of a sunrise after a long journey, and the quiet accumulation of wisdom that subtly transforms perspective. From serene sunsets mirrored on tropical waters to thoughtful exchanges that echo long after parting, every experience adds texture and depth, reminding me that travel is not merely movement through space but growth through connection and insight.

When I reflect on this journey, I'm struck by the lasting impressions left by the people I've met along the way. Their influence has been profound and humbling, revealing how deeply our lives intertwine. Childhood friendships forged on sunlit ball fields, shared melodies in the high school band,

and the tender lessons of young love all shaped my outlook in ways I still uncover. I remember, too, the teachers whose patience and dedication kindled curiosity — Mrs. Cross, whose sixth-grade classroom awakened my imagination; Mr. Sobak, whose chemistry lessons challenged my thinking; and Mrs. Buffington, whose steadfast support in mathematics built my confidence. Their guidance, and that of many mentors who followed, charted a path of lifelong learning that continues to this day.

Beyond the classroom, the world itself became my teacher. Encounters with technicians, professionals, and patients from a wide range of backgrounds revealed the beauty of human difference and the strength of shared humanity. Each conversation taught me empathy, each collaboration mutual respect. Friendships nurtured in adulthood — through shared challenges, laughter, and the passage of time — remain a source of joy and renewal. These connections, spanning local circles and far-reaching corners of the globe, remind me that true friendship knows no borders. To each person who has walked beside me, I offer heartfelt gratitude for the light and energy you've brought into my life.

Places, too, have a voice that lingers. Perhaps it began with my father's love for the open road, which stirred my own wanderlust at age four. I still recall the mist-veiled peaks of the Great Smoky Mountains, the living history of Williamsburg, the golden warmth of Florida's beaches, and the thrill of my first New England snowstorm. Our great family treks westward in 1956 and 1965 unfolded like chapters of an epic, revealing the breathtaking scale and spirit of the American landscape. Those journeys sparked a lifelong passion to explore and to witness the beauty and diversity that define our nation. I have since been blessed to visit all fifty states — each one unique, each a reflection of the strength and story of America.

My curiosity carried me far beyond my homeland as well—toward places I once only dreamed of. Across Asia, I found lessons in both difference and unity. Japan's harmony of tradition and innovation, the Philippines' warmth and resilience, Malaysia's vibrant cultures, Nepal's spiritual calm, and Cambodia's solemn history each offered insight into the enduring power of human spirit. These travels also deepened my appreciation for the work of Kiwanians across the Asia-Pacific—selfless individuals serving communities with compassion and purpose. Their example reaffirmed the shared values that link us all.

Latin America, too, revealed histories layered with resilience and creativity. Though my visits there were brief, they sparked a desire to return and explore the region's rich cultural rhythms more deeply.

Europe continues to draw me with its timeless charm. From Tuscany's rolling vineyards to the snow-dusted peaks of the Swiss Alps, each landscape tells its own story. My "Danish sister" has welcomed me time and again with warmth that turns every visit into a homecoming. The hearty comfort of German dishes—savory sausages, creamy potatoes, tangy sauerkraut, and a frothy glass of beer—stirs the same sense of belonging. Walking ancestral paths across the continent reminds me of my roots, grounding me in gratitude and stirring a familiar longing to return.

The sea, too, calls to me with its rhythm and mystery. Life aboard a great ship, where the horizon stretches endlessly and each sunrise heralds a new shore, awakens a deep sense of adventure. Ocean voyages offer not only vistas of distant lands but the gift of human connection—fellow travelers whose stories enrich the journey. I've shared decks and dinners with a British poultry farmer, a Chinese aristocrat, a locomotive designer, a Swiss air-traffic executive, a Holocaust survivor, and a Midwestern pastor. Each conversation widened my view of the human story. The crew—drawn from Poland, South Africa, the Philippines, and beyond—taught me that though our backgrounds differ, our hopes and joys are often the same.

Across more than seventy-five years, these people, places, and moments have shaped my life's narrative. Though no single page could contain every memory, each encounter has left a lasting imprint—lessons in gratitude, humility, and wonder that continue to guide me.

As Yogi Berra once said, "Life is a learning experience, but only if you learn." And so, I look ahead with anticipation—to the next path, the next sunrise, the next conversation that will deepen my understanding and continue this lifelong journey of discovery.

Around the Next Bend

"Travel makes one modest. You see what a tiny place you occupy in the world"
— Gustave Flaubert, French Writer

Roads beckon, where vibrant visions gleam,
Landscapes shift and sway within a waking dream.
Prairies and canyons rise, framing a world untold,
What mysteries await, what stories will unfold?

Valleys cradle towns, where shadows softly creep,
From lofty mountain slopes, where ancient secrets sleep.
Fenced fields and farms keep a tranquil, steady beat,
What beauty thrives, where nature's wonders meet?

Desert dawn explodes, in colors bold and bright.
Rosy twilight lingers in soft and fading light.
Sunset paints the Western skies, a fleeting, vivid hue,
What phantom vistas wait, where dreams begin anew?

Rugged summits rise to pierce the vast and endless sky.
Eagles guard the peaks, where hawks and breezes fly.
Regal elk graze calmly in meadows, bathed in golden rays,
What wild scenes awaken, in nature's mystic ways?

Mountains yield to shores, where sea and land collide.
Wharves hum with life, where sea captains bravely ride.
Old watermen weave tales of tides and the ocean's might.
What faces greet us in the dying evening light?

Sun-drenched parks resonate with joy, as children play,
City streets unfold, where urban tales hold sway.
Grand boulevards unveil vistas, we are wary to depart,
What urban rhythms quicken the eager heart?

Yesterday's rich echoes, each gentle and strong,
Recall journeys, etched in time, the past lingers long.
Where will pathways lead, each greeting us with cheer,
What travel melodies chime, as new adventures near?

Down memory lane, past destinations gleam,
A lifetime of stirring journeys form a traveler's dream.
Each magical recollection yields a priceless dividend.
Time to plan, what adventure waits around the next bend?

The Frosting of Life

"The true harvest of my life is intangible — a little star dust caught, a portion of the rainbow I have clutched."
— Henry David Thoreau, American Naturalist

In earlier chapters, I shared the essential building blocks of my life: family, faith, and meaningful relationships. Others may find fulfillment in rewarding work, thrilling adventures, or financial security that exceeds basic needs. These form the layers of the cake — the solid foundation that provides structure and sustenance.

I have partaken in those layers and found joy in them. Yet, if life is to be genuinely savored, it must offer more than the basics. It needs the sweet, intangible *frosting* — the experiences that nourish the soul and elevate the ordinary into something extraordinary.

Thoreau beautifully expressed the essence of stardust and rainbows — those fleeting, luminous bursts of beauty that rise above the mundane. I see them as life's enchanting *frosting*, transforming mere existence into a vivid masterpiece of emotion and sensation. Every moment, whether crafted by human hands or gifted by nature, enriches our days with wonder, tenderness, and joy.

Music, for me, stands as the purest form of these intangible treasures. Plato once wrote, "Music gives a soul to the universe, wings to the mind, flight to the imagination, and life to everything." I wholeheartedly agree. From the grandeur of a symphony's crescendo to the heartfelt twang of a country ballad, music has the power to stir something deep within me.

Classical compositions carry the weight and majesty of history, while the familiar harmonies of 1960s pop songs transport me to the carefree days of youth. Music—no matter the genre—can inspire through lyrics or soothe through melody. Country music, with its tales of hard work and heritage, resonates with the enduring spirit of our nation. Meanwhile, orchestral scores and the reverent tones of a pipe organ paint vivid portraits in the mind. Each style reaffirms Henry Wadsworth Longfellow's timeless words: *music is the universal language of mankind.*

Whether I am standing on a cruise ship deck, gazing across the endless expanse of ocean, or hiking beneath the towering peaks of the Grand Tetons with my iPod® playing softly in my ears, music revitalizes my spirit. It adds an invisible layer of magic to every moment, awakening gratitude for the simple act of being alive.

Closely following music is the pleasure of a thoughtfully prepared meal. It need not involve elaborate artistry or exotic ingredients—only care, tradition, and authenticity. The comforting aroma of my grandmother's fried chicken and freshly baked bread, the rich flavors from my mother's New England heritage, and the time-honored recipes passed through generations all delight my senses.

Vickie mastered the art of family favorites by weaving together the culinary wisdom inherited from her mother and borrowed from mine. Though I prefer home cooking and its familiar tastes, my travels have broadened my palate. German and Italian cuisines, in particular, have deepened my appreciation for the connection between food, culture, and memory. Together, these experiences form a kind of culinary *frosting*—one that nourishes both body and soul.

Art, too, contributes its own sweetness to life. The beauty of great artwork has an almost spiritual impact on me. Though I lack the trained eye of an expert, I am deeply moved by the power of artistic expression. Standing before the *Mona Lisa*, I was transfixed by her immortal smile and the quiet serenity of her gaze.

In contrast, the monumental scale and intricate detail of da Vinci's *Last Supper* evoke reverence and awe. The disciples' faces reflect the gravity of the moment, for we, as witnesses, know the suffering that lies ahead. Rembrandt's *Sacrifice of Isaac* pierced me with raw emotion—the interplay of light and shadow captured the unbearable tension of faith tested by love. Isaac's pleading eyes and Abraham's trembling hand conveyed sorrow so real that my breath caught, until my gaze fell upon the angel's intervening hand. I left that gallery marked forever by the experience.

Yet even the most powerful creations of human hands pale beside the masterpieces of nature. Mother Nature's artistry knows no bounds. From the vast grandeur of Yellowstone National Park to the tranquil mirror of Holland Lake, from the meandering Rhone River to the rhythmic roar of the South Australian coast, her wonders never fail to replenish my spirit.

Every landscape holds its own poetry: the wildflowers in a Swiss meadow, the whispering wind through tall grass, the serenity of twilight settling over distant hills. And within these landscapes dwell the creatures that complete nature's harmony—the flash of crimson in a cardinal's wings, the commanding flight of an eagle, the quiet strength of an elephant, and the stealthy grace of a Bengal tiger.

The rhythm of the seasons offers its own chorus of beauty: the bright bloom of spring's daffodils, the golden glow of autumn, the crystalline stillness of freshly fallen snow. Each season adds its own *frosting* to the passage of time, reminding us that life's beauty is ever-changing and endlessly renewed — if only we choose to see it.

Like a child eagerly licking the icing from a cupcake — be it yellow cake with chocolate buttercream or spiced cake topped with caramel — we are instinctively drawn to life's sweetness. As we mature, we come to appreciate the balance between the cake and its frosting. The routines and responsibilities of daily life provide stability and purpose, but the intangible joys — music, art, nature, and shared moments of love — add the richness, depth, and texture that make life truly fulfilling.

May you, my children and grandchildren, learn to cherish both the essential and the beautiful. Seek not only what sustains you but also what uplifts you. In doing so, you will savor the full flavor of existence and create a lifetime of sweet, unforgettable memories.

Lady Liberty

Liberty has never come from government... Liberty has always come from the subjects of it. The history of liberty is the history of resistance. The history of liberty is a history of limitations of governmental power, not the increase of it."
— Woodrow Wilson, United States President

In New York Harbor, a proud lady stands,
A beacon of hope shining across the lands.
Her golden torch casts a radiant gleam,
Guiding lost souls searching for a dream.

She shepherds strangers from strife they flee,
Yearning for life, self-determined and free.
A promise of living, fueled by freedom's desire,
Satisfied by achievement, ignited by fire.

She watches citizens returning home once more,
Realizing liberty's strength, through sun and downpour.
Reflecting on settlers who arrived from strange shores,
Persecuted pilgrims determined to open religious doors.

Colonists landing south, heard opportunity's call,
Erecting foundations for freedom, standing tall.

Miss Liberty remembers the many sacrifices made,
Shaping a nation with principles that won't fade.

No autocrat reigns; a federal republic stands bold,
With founding visions, the principles won't grow old.
Washington, Jefferson, and Henry's fervent plea,
Adams, Franklin, and Madison, beacons of liberty.

She witnessed Lewis and Clark exploring frontier's domain,
Followed by settlers forging lives while enduring pain.
To preserve the Union, with emancipation's light.
Lincoln demanded universal freedom and led the fight.

When threatened by foes from faraway, she wept,
Enduring many troubling years, she stood erect.
Patriots from cities, prairies, and plains went to defend,
Determined, brave, and strong, they fought to the end.

Led by Pershing, Eisenhower, and Marshall's global sway,
While MacArthur, Patton, and Bradley battled each day.
In the field, GI Joe stood firm throughout the land,
At home, production surged, led by Rosie's steady hand.

Looking west, vast domains stretched beyond Hudson's flow,
Diverse regions, resource-rich, impacting tomorrow.
The South's warm spirit combined with hospitality and grace.
Echoes of Williamsburg's past, which time cannot erase.

Self-reliant farmers reliably tend the fertile soil,
Harvesting bounty through endless loyal toil.
Endless days reveal cowhands shaping the West.
With regions uniting, the nation is blessed.

Lady Liberty smiles at our greatest power,
It's found in her people and their willpower.
Descendants of a myriad of heritages, free from their fears,
Pursuing individual dreams, laboring through the years.

Citizens respecting their neighbors' hopes and dreams,
Worshipping their God, while avoiding life's extremes.
Artists of all ilk, focus on the nation's heart and soul.
Laborers, teachers, those who serve, keep the country whole.

A tear in her eye appears when she sees Liberty's plight,
Fraud, theft, and disregard of the law dim her light.
Freedom demands responsibility; we must embrace,
Following Lady Liberty's path, we will sustain this place.

The symbol of Liberty stares into the future of this land,
Her confidence is bound to principles on which we stand.
Constitutionally bound, a declaration that we recall,
Granted Independence, sovereignty, and freedom for all.

THE CANYON SPEAKS

"Leave it as it is. The ages have been at work on it, and man can only mar it."
— Theodore Roosevelt, United States President and American Naturalist

Ancient majestic spires centuries old,
Stand vigilant 'bove the canyon's shaded deep.
Vivid hues brush cliffs with colors bold,
Where timeless secrets in the darkness sleep.

The river flows, nature's patient hand.
Chiseling crimson gorges through ancient stone.
Coral cliffs silently frame superb vistas grand.
Revealing a spectrum of colors divinely sown.

The canyon whispers legends to hearts that hear,
Lore of ages past, inscribed on each weathered face.
Revealing forgotten truths, both far and near,
Stories of generations past, thought lost in space.

The quiet dawn unveils tales it holds dear,
Innocence shared beneath an endless sky.
Broken promises linger in twilight's violet sphere,
While shadows of secrets ponder softly, why?

Truths shimmer in the ripples of emerald streams,
Bright as the bloom of the desert's cactus flower.
Memories glow, vibrant like sunlight beams,
Each a statement to the vastness of nature's power.

In canyon's depths, tomorrow's promise lies,
As beautiful and bold as golden canyon walls.
Limitless horizons, reaching for celestial skies,
Nature's testament, revealed as God calls.

Magical Mountains

"The mountains are calling, and I must go."
— John Muir, Naturalist

There's magic woven in mountains' grace,
  A yearning call that beckons us to trace.
  Why do I feel the pull, by a force unnamed?
To distant peaks that remain wild and untamed.

Wild mysteries, centuries old, veiled in rugged stone,
  Open to wanderers, like me, seeking the unknown.
  What vistas await where valley winds have blown?
A tranquil haven, a sanctuary for spirits, divinely known.

Emerald meadows shimmer like jewels aglow,
  Nestled among peaks, where wild spirits flow.
  How will this sanctuary shape the essence of me?
This wilderness inspires my soul, setting my heart free.

In dawn's stillness, intense aspirations ignite,
  Reflections of dreams, painted by nature's light.
  How will God's wonders unfold before my eyes?
By chilly winds and serenading birds, beneath blue skies.

Promising an eternal bridge, where earth and sky meet,
Magical mountains, steadfast, await my returning feet.
What draws me back to the mountains' regal embrace?
To savor their majesty, a connection to God's Grace.

Shoebox in the Attic

"Youth comes but once in a lifetime."
— Henry Wadsworth Longfellow, American Poet

There is a shoebox in the attic that sleeps,
Buried in a dark corner, old memories it keeps.
Dust guards the treasures from bygone years,
Knick-knacks, pictures, and forgotten souvenirs.

Bulging, crumbling sides with a lid askew,
Gradually collapsing due to aging glue.
Its sides tell a story of time's slow creep.
Rarely disturbed, each image runs deep.

Teenage tokens reflecting laughter and tears,
Collections of joy that resonate through the years.
Faded baseball cards of heroes once grand,
Trinkets recall autumn's football bands.

Worn-out baseball gloves once worn in sunlit haze,
Before the world's more hectic ways.
Memories of summer games and shagging flies,
Before, girls were attracted to guys wearing ties.

Curios saved from carefree youthful nights,
Prom dates and goodbyes, in fading lights.
Not mere clutter, but fragments held dear,
Mosaic mementos, life's treasures sincere.

There is a shoebox in the attic, mine alone.
A rustic capsule guarding the memory zone.
Lift the lid, and let the past come alive,
Memories of yesteryear with a tear in my eye.

Passing Memories

"We don't remember days, we remember moments."
— Cesare Pavese, Italian Novelist and Poet

Uninvited memories of long ago, like restless ghosts, take flight,
Yesterday's forgotten images invade my mind and come to light.
A sudden color, a neglected tune, a whisper from the past,
Special moments, lost to time, flash like lightning and reemerge at last.

Slivers of time, faces and scenes, from places long erased,
Emerge from memories' depths, where fleeting moments are traced.
Childhood's fervor, the noise of endless, carefree days,
Backyard games and Saturday matinees, our youthful hearts ablaze.

Summer afternoons on shiny bikes, we roamed sunlit streets,
With rivers and valleys calling, where nature and freedom meet.
But seasons evaporate; childhood chaos slowly wanes,
As new paths bloom ahead, where dreams and ideals reign.

Beyond the red bike's gleam, a car's sleek chrome awaits,
A wider world unfolds in a broader parking space.
A silver Pontiac roams as rock 'n' roll refrains take hold,
Date nights blossom, recalling stories waiting to be told.

Sheltered days fade as teen years arrive so fast,
Responsibilities loom, part-time jobs, high school's a blast.
Time accelerates, transforming wishes into teenage schemes,
Unseen hurdles and growing pains, land hard—at least it seems.

Life's first romance glows: a second date, would she say yes?
Her head on my shoulder, a wink igniting evening's caress.
Moments where romantic whispers linger, yet remain unclear,
Her lavender dress frames a blue-eyed beauty, forever dear.

An October breeze wraps us in warmth beneath the autumn sky,
Strolling hand-in-hand on date nights as tender moments pass by.
Silver screen stars spark our frequent movie nights,
And occasionally, theaters called to see stars above stage lights.

Cherished days long gone—I escorted the homecoming queen,
We danced beneath starlit skies, welcoming dawn's first beam.

Memories retell shared times, etched on life's gentle page,
Funny how visions and dreams converge upon life's stage.

Time, the healer, softens farewells' sharp-edged sting,
As love departs, new chapters emerge with the arrival of spring.
Time teaches that brief encounters yield to life's winding way,
Yet ageless days light the path, blending the best of yesterday.

A channel in love's river, wide and deep, will bloom,
Carrying us to futures unknown, far from gloom.
Hope lights our trail, a guiding star, steadfast and true,
True love grows from lessons learned, anchored in a heart anew.

LOVE

Four Little Letters

"Life is a flower of which love is the honey."
— Victor Hugo, French Writer

"L-O-V-E," is it a gift, a challenge, or a storm?
A sudden tempest or a hand to keep us warm?
Perhaps the refreshment of a gentle rain on earth's face,
Surely a child's innocent laugh, a gentle first embrace.

Where does love dwell? In a giving, calloused hand,
Or within the brilliant gold of a loving wedding band.
It hides in soft caresses, in shared quiet space,
A flickering candle in time's relentless race.

When does it bloom? In the midnight's, tear-stained plea,
In the promise of sunrises, wild and fiercely free.
In hearts that seek truth, where melodies sing,
In kindness of the sweetest gifts that love can bring.

When is it felt? When the heart is open wide,
Overflowing in family bonds, where trust resides.
In the vibrant pulse of life, even in shared pain,
Through every heartbeat, love helps us rise again.

What is love's touch? A soft sunlight's gleam,
In love's first touch, a youth's vibrant dream.
In intimate vows, a lifetime's flowing stream,
Moments of grace, where love's pure waters teem.

How powerful is love? Compelling it can transform,
An enduring bond to weather any storm.
Unconditional devotion in the winds ever bending,
Selfless sacrifice, dedication, never-ending.

What is the greatest love? The gift of Grace.
God's supreme touch penetrates every space.
The spice of love is lost without God's love.
Eternally conceived, sent on the wings of a dove.

LIFE OF LOVE

"There is no remedy for love but to love more."
— Henry David Thoreau, American Naturalist

People crave love through smiles and tears.
Children seek comfort from encircling fears.
Mature love cushions from life's sting.
As souls grasp for enduring love in the abundant spring.
Yet doubt creeps in, a love of acceptance we need,
To banish the shadows where insecurities breed.

Love engulfs the spirit in countless ways.
It arrives riding sunlight's golden rays.
Unexpectedly, it invades through a gentle embrace,
Or lingers in twilight, behind nightfall's shadowy lace.
No one knows when love will show its face.
A glance can ignite a soul or quicken a heart's pace.

Young love sparkles with radiant promise,
Resilient with hope without compromise.
It can overcome shyness, as experience takes flight.
But when betrayed, injured hearts are dark as night.
Shattered dreams linger, promises once sweet,
Lost in the rhythm of love's bitter-sweet beat.

Bruised souls yearn for a healing that is true,
Seeking devoted love in place of what was once blue.
Searching through the darkness for meaning,
Praying silently for a chance at a new beginning.
A fresh start fostered on a foundation of trust,
Abandoning bonds no stronger than stardust.

Patient love grows, revealing warmth of abundance,
Devotion grows through long-standing romance.
Forever committed, growing stronger each day.
Boundless affection in every word, in every way.
An enduring union entwined at its core,
With love's endless power, we both can soar.

Love, empowered by God's unfailing Grace,
A gentle approval shining on His face.
Reinforced with the sunrise of each new day.
Walking in faith, love's joy is enhanced as we pray.
A life of love guided by God's holy light.
Together we flourish, our hearts glowing bright.

An Invitation from God

"There is no more lovely, friendly, and charming relationship, communion, or company than a good marriage."
— Martin Luther, German Theologian

A beautifully engraved wedding invitation heralds more than a date and time — it announces a sacred celebration, the culmination of a love that longs to share a lifetime. It represents countless hours of planning and anticipation, leading to a day filled with magic, gratitude, and the promise of cherished memories.

When my niece asked me to officiate her ceremony, I was profoundly honored. Agreeing to officiate transformed the family gathering into a deeply meaningful spiritual experience for me.

My love and respect for my niece and her sisters made the responsibility even greater. I wanted my words to resonate not only with the couple but with everyone present. My goal was to preserve the sanctity of the ceremony, uphold the solemnity of their vows, and honor the bride's heartfelt request — to speak about *the significance of being joined together as life partners.* Her trust touched me deeply. I sensed that her request reflected the examples of enduring commitment she had witnessed — between her grandparents, and between Vickie and me.

The word **"partner"** is central. A wedding day marks the beginning of a sacred partnership, one grounded in love and mutual respect. Though poets, musicians, and artists throughout the ages have tried to capture its mystery, love remains beautifully elusive — a force that cannot be confined to words alone.

Christian psychologist Larry Crabb once wrote of a love that enables couples "to endure wrong with patience, resist evil with conviction, enjoy the good times with gusto, give richly of themselves with humility, and nourish each other's soul."

And, of course, the timeless words of St. Paul in *1 Corinthians 13* remain the gold standard for understanding true love:

"Love is patient, love is kind. It does not envy, it does not boast, it is not proud. It is not rude, it is not self-seeking, it is not easily angered; it keeps no record of wrongs. Love does not delight in evil but rejoices with the truth. It always protects, always trusts, always hopes, always perseveres."

These words form the blueprint of a thriving partnership — one sustained not only by affection but by faith, humility, and grace.

To these timeless truths, I would like to add three personal observations that life and experience have taught me:

1. Embrace change together.

Life's path seldom follows a straight line. Detours and unexpected turns are inevitable — some filled with joy, others with challenge. The key is to face them as one. Lean on each other for strength, and remember that you can draw upon the love and support of family and friends when the journey feels uncertain.

2. Foster individual growth.

A healthy marriage allows space for each partner to flourish. Encourage your partner's dreams and personal calling, even when they lead in new directions. Supporting one another's growth enriches not only the individual but also the union you share.

3. Give more than you take.

Marriage is not a 50-50 arrangement. There will be times when one partner must go the extra mile. Acts of selfless love, freely given, yield immeasurable rewards. Keep no ledger of effort or sacrifice — love thrives when giving becomes its own joy.

These principles may sound simple, but living them requires strength rooted in faith and a trust that God's hand is always at work. As Paul's letter to the Ephesians reminds us,

"Be imitators of God, therefore, as dearly loved children, and live a life of love, just as Christ loved us..."

A wedding invitation, then, is also an invitation from God Himself — a divine summons to allow the Holy Spirit to rejuvenate and sustain your marriage. When you accept that invitation, your faith deepens, your experience of grace expands, and your family bonds are strengthened.

Each wedding invitation you receive is more than a call to celebrate love between two people — it is God's reminder to include Him at your table, to let His presence dwell at the center of your shared life.

A wedding marks the beginning of a remarkable journey. Let Christ's message of love be your guiding light. He will walk beside you through every joy, every trial, and every opportunity that life presents. When you respond "Yes" to God's invitation through Christ, He accompanies you every step of the way.

My earnest prayer for every couple is this:

May your love grow like a mighty tree — roots deep, branches high — revealing new beauty in every season.

May you dare to dream beyond imagination.

May you find joy and courage in discovering who you are and where God is leading you.

May your partnership reflect your shared mission and reveal the endless possibilities of love lived faithfully.

AMEN

My Special Angel

"When angels visit us, we do not hear the rustle of wings, nor feel the feathery touch of the breast of a dove; but we know their presence by the love they create in our hearts."
— Mary Baker Eddy, American Religious Leader

To: Vickie Lynn Wicks Riley

Each morning when we awaken, we cannot know what the day will bring. Some days unfold gently, while others quietly alter the course of our lives. October 4, 1968 — the day of our first date — was one of those extraordinary days. I could never have imagined then how beautifully our story would unfold, shaping decades of happiness grounded in love, respect, and unwavering devotion.

Our courtship began with a movie, *The Bliss of Mrs. Blossom*, and dinner at Cy Bloom's *Place in the Alley*. I remember being struck by your radiant smile — it convinced me to ask for a second date at the University of Maryland Homecoming game. We laughed as the rain poured from kick-off to the final whistle, soaking us both but sealing a memory we would cherish forever.

After that weekend, our time together grew naturally, until I could no longer envision life without you. You were different from anyone I had ever met — thoughtful, grounded, and patient. Unlike others who sought an early commitment before I completed pharmacy school, you understood and shared my conviction to finish our education before taking the next step. That shared belief laid the foundation for everything that followed.

No letter could ever fully capture the ways you have shaped my life and our family. Your love has been a compass — guiding, steadying, and sustaining. You carried the greatest share of nurturing our three children, Aileen, Kimberly, and Kevin, tailoring your guidance to meet each of their unique needs. You were mother, counselor, teacher, and faith advocate all in one. Because of your devotion, I was able to serve as a pharmacist, the calling that defined my professional life.

You never once complained about my long hours or midnight pharmacy calls. Later, when you returned to the classroom to further your own education, you did so selflessly, ensuring our children could pursue theirs. Your perseverance and grace gave our family stability and opportunity.

You also stood beside me through every professional transition — encouraging my early position at the University of Maryland Hospital and supporting the venture that became Washington Heights Pharmacy. I still remember the evenings when you brought me supper at work, your quiet presence lifting my spirits more than you knew. Over my 53-year career, your steadfast encouragement was the constant that made every challenge bearable and every success meaningful.

You embraced our family vacations with enthusiasm, giving me precious, uninterrupted time with our children. Those shared adventures have become the heart of my fondest memories. You endured my countless travel ideas with humor and patience, and together we discovered the world — from the rigid atmosphere of the Soviet Union in 1973 to the breathtaking mountains of Nepal. Each journey deepened our faith and strengthened our bond, especially as we visited sacred places that renewed our spiritual connection.

Your contributions extended even to my ministry. You spent hours editing and refining the sermons I wrote as a lay speaker, helping me express God's Word more clearly. You may not realize it, but those quiet hours of study and reflection deepened my understanding of Christ's teachings and enriched my spiritual life beyond measure.

When the children began building their own lives, you encouraged my participation in Kiwanis — opening another chapter of service and shared adventure. Together, we met remarkable people and witnessed corners of the world we had never dreamed of seeing. Through it all, your love made each experience extraordinary.

My life has been immeasurably blessed because of you. Our story has seen sunshine and storms, straight paths and steep climbs, yet every turn has been illuminated by your love. You are my partner, my constant friend, a wonderful wife, and an extraordinary mother.

Our years together have yielded a lifetime of memories — enough to fill volumes — yet no words can ever fully express the gratitude and love I feel for you. Your companionship is the greatest gift I've ever known. If I have given you even a fraction of what you have given me, then my heart is content.

With all my love,

Your husband and partner,

Art

Reflections

Yesterday, Today, and Tomorrow

"Learn from yesterday, live for today, hope for tomorrow. The important thing is not to stop questioning."
— Albert Einstein, Theoretical physicist

Time flows relentlessly through yesterday, today, and tomorrow. Each carries its own distinct panorama, shaping the unfolding journey of our lives.

Yesterday's landscape reveals memories both luminous and shadowed—moments that will never be duplicated. Today exposes fields ripe for cultivation, while tomorrow stretches before us as an uncharted horizon shimmering with limitless potential.

Yesterday's view juggles echoes, whispers, and remnants of emotion. Like the tender strains of *"Yesterday"* by the Beatles, it evokes a bittersweet nostalgia that nourishes the soul. Within its frame dwell the warmth of cherished laughter, the faces of those we've loved and lost, and the sting of missed chances or opportunities not seized.

For me, yesterday is a gallery of sun-drenched afternoons and evenings bathed in October's silver moonlight. It's alive with youthful escapades and the indelible imprints of significant souls. I document these memories not as fading relics but as guiding stars—illuminations for future generations. May they shine brightly on the paths of those who follow, encouraging them to seize their own moments before they, too, become yesterdays.

Today, in contrast, is a fleeting opportunity—an open field shimmering with fragile, precious jewels waiting to be shaped into reality. Before it slips into history, we face a choice: to squander the hours on trivial pursuits or to cultivate a garden of purpose.

Each dawn brings with it the chance for a shift in perspective, a deliberate infusion of optimism that can transform the day ahead. When we choose to see through the lens of God's grace, the ordinary becomes sacred. We begin to recognize the talents, opportunities, and blessings placed before us. This grace empowers us to deepen our faith, discover new possibilities, and contribute meaningfully to the communities that surround us.

A gentle hand extended to a struggling friend, a listening ear offered to an uncertain teenager, or a moment of wisdom shared with a grandchild—these small acts ripple outward, reflecting divine love and leaving behind a life well-lived.

Today also calls upon us to awaken our creative spirits—to paint, compose, craft, and mold beauty into the world. Art and music, often undervalued, enrich our souls and tether us to the shared human experience. To stand before a timeless masterpiece in a museum is to hear the artist's voice across the centuries. A melody can shift the atmosphere of a day, soothing or inspiring us in ways words cannot.

God-given talents are meant to be activated, shared, and woven into the greater fabric of humanity. They extend far beyond the arts; they include every ability and passion bestowed upon us. Our sacred responsibility is to uncover and nurture these gifts, allowing them to flourish.

These are the ways we invest our time today. God grants each of us only a finite number of days, and too often we reach the end of one realizing we have not fully explored its possibilities. To waste the precious gift of time is to disappoint the Giver Himself. Therefore, let us pledge to make wiser use of our time—to shape today into a bridge toward the future we long to create.

Tomorrow stretches before us like a meadow of infinite beauty and boundless promise. Yet how we approach it depends upon our mindset.

The first perspective is fear—a prism that casts a shadow of gloom, smothering potential beneath anxiety and apprehension. Such fear not only stifles our spirit but also seeps into the hearts of those around us.

The second is indifference—an apathetic resignation that assumes destiny lies beyond our control. This perspective blinds us to the orchard of opportunity that surrounds us, keeping us from harvesting its fruit.

The third, and most powerful, is hope—a vision of an expansive grove of opportunity that ignites the soul with anticipation. Tomorrow is an unharvested gift, a blank canvas awaiting our strokes, a melody waiting to be composed.

It calls us to explore horizons in every direction—to the north, south, east, and west. The compass of purpose points us toward acts of service, deeper faith, uncharted journeys, and the enduring lessons of history. These experiences broaden our vision, enrich our understanding, and cultivate wisdom.

Let yesterday be a teacher, today a foundation, and tomorrow a masterpiece. Learn from the echoes of the past, invest wisely in the present, and craft a future that resonates with purpose and grace.

Yesterday is gone. Today is swiftly becoming history. Tomorrow's promise is closer than you think. The memories we create in this very moment will one day become the yesterdays of those who follow—a legacy that transcends time.

In the Rearview Mirror

"Life can only be understood backwards; but it must be lived forwards."
— Søren Kierkegaard, Danish Philosopher

Albert Einstein once reflected, "Each of us is here for a brief sojourn; for what purpose we know not, though sometimes we sense it. But without deeper reflection, one knows from daily life that one exists for other people."

Throughout my life, I have sought to live by that belief — serving others through my profession and my community, learning from every encounter, and recognizing how each moment has quietly shaped me. As I now peer into the rearview mirror of my life, I see not merely the passage of years but the vast array of experiences that have left lasting impressions on my heart and mind. Each reflection calls me to gratitude and a deeper understanding of the many influences that have guided my journey.

Travel has long been one of my greatest passions — a source of discovery, perspective, and renewal that my family has graciously indulged. After every adventure, I am inevitably asked the same question: "What place or country do you like best?"

The answer, of course, is impossible. Each destination possesses its own magic — its own language of beauty, tradition, and wonder. Traveling frees me from the ordinary rhythm of daily life, immersing me in the colors and textures of the world. Among my fondest memories is the breathtaking sight of sunrise from the deck of a cruise ship, where the first golden light spilled across the horizon, igniting the sea in hues of amber and rose. Rising early to greet the dawn has always stirred something within me — the quiet assurance that no matter how turbulent life becomes, the world continues to turn toward new beginnings.

At the pinnacle of my travel recollections stands the memory of a mountain summit in the Gallatin National Forest, where I stood surrounded by the grandeur of creation. From that high vantage point, the land unfolded in waves of green and gold — the mountains solemn and proud, the rivers twisting like silver threads, the forests alive with elk and bison moving through the vast wilderness of the greater Yellowstone ecosystem.

By contrast, the Green Mountains of Vermont offer gentler beauty. I remember sitting with a bottle of wine and a wedge of local cheese, overlooking the quiet village of Stowe. The hum of nature surrounded me — the rustle of trees, the distant chirp of birds — and as the sun descended, the sky blazed in shades of violet and crimson. Each sunset felt like a promise that tomorrow would arrive carrying its own small miracles.

Tomorrow, I might find myself in Hawaii, watching a rainbow stretch across the sky after a fleeting mauka shower. The islands, shaped by wind and tide, whisper stories of their earliest settlers — the Polynesians who honored the sea and the land as sacred kin. Yet Hawaii is but one of many places that have touched my heart. I have been moved by the green splendor of Ireland, the hearty traditions of Germany, and the ancient mystery of Turkey — each culture enriching my soul in ways words can barely hold.

In Ireland, I felt instantly at home. The rolling emerald hills and the laughter of the people seemed to speak the same language as my spirit. Their warmth enveloped me like an old friend's embrace. I wandered through cobblestoned streets lined with centuries-old buildings, paused in cozy pubs filled with song and laughter, and listened to stories told with that uniquely Irish gift for turning memory into music. Savoring a pint of local beer or a bowl of soup beside a crackling fire, I found beauty in simplicity and in the enduring spirit of community.

Germany—especially Bavaria—felt like returning to something familiar, as though my ancestry whispered through each cobblestone and meal. I've always believed my German roots manifest most clearly through my appetite: bratwurst, sauerkraut, mashed potatoes, and the satisfying chill of a crisp beer. In Bavaria, every meal feels like a celebration. I recall climbing alpine trails, sharing fondue by a mountain window, tasting cheeses rich with the flavor of the valley, and ending the day with a decadent chocolate dessert. Each visit there feels like rediscovering a part of myself.

Traveling farther east, Turkey awakened my fascination with the intersection of history and faith. Istanbul and Ephesus remain etched in my mind. Walking through the marble streets of Ephesus, I could almost hear the echoes of ancient footsteps—feel the weight of history under my palms. Knowing that figures such as Mary, the mother of Jesus, and John, the apostle, once walked those same paths filled me with reverence.

Istanbul, with its blend of East and West, overwhelmed the senses—the scent of spices in the air, the call to prayer rolling through the city, the laughter of merchants, the taste of rich, unfamiliar dishes. One evening, as I cruised the Bosporus Strait, the lights of the city shimmered across the water like a constellation fallen to Earth. Palaces of sultans lined the banks, silent witnesses to centuries of empire and exchange. The next morning, the domes of the Blue Mosque and Hagia Sophia stood before me—testaments to human devotion and resilience.

Yet for all my global wanderings, my heart remains tethered to the story of my own homeland. Williamsburg, Virginia, never fails to stir something within me. There is a living pulse along Duke of Gloucester Street—a resonance of freedom and ambition. Walking among the preserved colonial buildings, I can almost hear Washington, Madison, Jefferson, and Henry debating in the glow of lantern light, wrestling with ideas that would shape a nation. Every visit to Williamsburg renews my awe for their courage and conviction, their willingness to risk everything for a vision of liberty.

As I glance again into that rearview mirror, the images that mean the most are not the landmarks or vistas—they are the faces of those who have journeyed beside me. The grandeur of nature is magnified by the laughter of companions; the beauty of distant cultures gains meaning through the kindness of their people.

In Cambodia, I met families who possessed little in material wealth yet overflowed with grace and generosity. Their smiles, radiant against the backdrop of hardship, reminded me that dignity and hope require no riches. In Nepal, I met artisans who carved and wove their heritage into every creation—their hands shaping beauty out of devotion. Encounters like these revealed that humanity's truest art is resilience.

Still, no experience compares to the love and joy shared with my family and friends. Their presence is the melody that gives life its harmony. I treasure the memory of standing with my wife beneath the towering majesty of Mount Rainier, feeling both small and infinite within its shadow. I can still see my daughter Aileen's face light up with courage as she conquered her fear on the Grizzly River Rampage at Opryland, laughter mingling with the roar of the water. I recall Kimberly's radiant smile during a sunlit picnic in the West, her joy bright as the afternoon sky. And I hold dear the morning my son Kevin and

I shared a sunrise in Bryce Canyon—the world bathed in gold, silence broken only by our quiet awe.

My memories spill over like an overflowing river—holidays, ball games, family gatherings, each one distinct and irreplaceable. I recall the laughter shared with my Danish sister and the warmth of welcoming exchange students from Finland and Switzerland into our home. These moments—simple, human, full of laughter—are the true currency of a life well-lived.

Author Tara Stiles once compared life's joys to drifting clouds: transient, luminous, and ever-changing. Through reflection, we weave these fleeting experiences into the fabric of meaning. Looking back, my life feels adorned with vivid colors—from the carefree dances of youth to the quiet, soul-deep connections forged with loved ones.

And so, as I look once more into the rearview mirror of my life, I understand that the journey itself has been the true destination. Each memory—bright or shadowed—has shaped who I am. The brilliance of joy and the softer hues of struggle coexist, forming a portrait of gratitude.

For in the end, it is not where we have traveled that defines us, but how deeply we have felt along the way.

The Future Must Start Today

"You cannot escape the responsibility of tomorrow by evading it today."
— Abraham Lincoln, United States President

History books bear witness to both the soaring triumphs and the sobering failures of humanity. Between these pages lie stories of those who dared to dream, who, with unwavering resolve, sought to shape the future. Their motives varied, from the intrepid Marco Polo, who bridged East and West through trade and understanding, to the visionary Christopher Columbus, who, seeking new trade routes to Asia, altered the course of world history. The human spirit has always craved adventure and progress, and the quest for a better future has been our driving force.

Two and a half centuries after Columbus's arrival in the Americas, a group of settlers landed on the banks of the James River in 1607, establishing Jamestown, Virginia. They arrived seeking opportunity as loyal subjects of the British crown, yet as the next sixteen decades unfolded, they were forced to confront the stark realities of living under a distant, unresponsive government, a monarch's arbitrary rule, and a parliament that prioritized conflicts over the needs of its colonies. The colonists, however, were a diverse group— farmers, skilled artisans, visionary leaders, and daring explorers—each bringing their unique backgrounds and experiences to this new land. Their shared purpose was clear: to carve out a new life in an uncharted territory.

Their efforts laid the foundation for a vibrant community, one rich in culture and innovation, as they faced the challenges of an unfamiliar environment. From aristocratic landowners to humble farmers, they gradually awakened to the promise of self-determination. The dream of a participatory government, independent of England, simmered throughout the mid-eighteenth century.

In the streets of Boston, Annapolis, New York, and Williamsburg, discontent began to grow, eventually blossoming into a revolutionary spirit. Patriots, driven by conviction, began to challenge the British Parliament's edicts, such as the Stamp Act, and to push back against the status quo. British military actions in Virginia and Massachusetts only served to amplify the call for rebellion. Though they knew the formidable challenges ahead—fighting against the power of a distant empire and the resistance of those loyal to the crown—the colonists dared to imagine a future of prosperity, collaboration, and individual liberties.

Despite the challenges and the voices of those who doubted their ability to govern themselves, patriots remained steadfast in their vision. Their aspirations culminated in the birth of the United States of America, an experiment in governance unlike any the world had seen. This bold new venture set the stage for the nation's future—a future built on self-determination, freedom, and the promise of equality for all.

For over two centuries, this experiment has endured, balancing the needs of its less populated states and striving to ensure equality for all citizens. The nation has weathered civil wars, political turmoil, global conflicts, and the rapid rise of technology. With each generation, the challenges of preserving and strengthening citizen-responsive institutions have been met. At the heart of these institutions is the federal government, which, according to the principles laid out in the Constitution, exists with the approval and support of the people.

The Constitution, forged in the heat of revolution, outlines the government's authority, responsibilities, and limitations. It is the product of hours of debate and compromise among the delegates who gathered in Philadelphia, and it stands as a testament to their enduring wisdom. In the early years of the republic, the scope of federal power was debated, legislated, and clarified by the Supreme Court. What emerged was a system that has served as a beacon of stability and liberty for nations worldwide.

Having traveled abroad, I have seen firsthand the contrast between the freedoms enjoyed by Americans and the struggles faced by citizens in poorer nations or those living under authoritarian regimes. These experiences compel me to speak out, for I have concluded that if the United States is to not only survive but flourish, we must remain true to the foundational principles enshrined in the Constitution. Our major institutions—government, education, and the press—must uphold the responsibilities granted to them by the American people.

Currently, these institutions increasingly prioritize their own power and prestige over serving the people. The Constitution is a sacred compact between the government and its citizens, defining the responsibilities of the federal government, the duties of the states, and the rights of the people. Allowing this delicate balance of power to be compromised by concentrating it in the hands of a few betrays the very essence of our republic.

The founders of our nation understood the dangers of power and envisioned elected service as an honor, not a career. Power, like any addiction, breeds a hunger for more, which can lead to complacency and corruption. Long-term incumbents in office are not only more susceptible to corruption, but they also discourage citizen participation, stifling fresh ideas and leading to apathy among the electorate.

We, the citizens, are the guardians of our democracy. It is our responsibility to demand that our government fulfills its basic obligations: to protect and defend our nation, to be fiscally responsible, to be transparent with the electorate, to safeguard individual freedoms, and to resist the undue influence of special interests. Failing to uphold these obligations erodes public trust in government and undermines the very foundation of our nation.

The most pressing responsibility of our government is to protect the safety of its citizens from external threats. This duty, deeply etched in the annals of history, stands as a pillar of paramount importance. Equally crucial is the need for truthfulness in government. Elected officials must be transparent, presenting the full and complete picture to the public. The erosion of truth in public discourse poisons our communities, misguiding our youth into believing that dishonesty is acceptable. Truthfulness is the bedrock upon which trust is built, and the misuse of taxpayer dollars fractures the fiscal foundation of our nation.

In an increasingly complex world, one vastly different from the experiences of the 18th-century patriots, it is imperative that the government educates its citizens about the myriad of challenges we face today. We must be transparent about the ambitions and intentions of our adversaries, the ever-shifting geopolitical landscape, and the various forces that seek to undermine our influence and, in some cases, destroy the very fabric of our way of life. Concealing the truth is not only misleading—it is a disservice to the American people, whose strength and resilience have always stemmed from their informed participation in the national discourse. The immense investments made by authoritarian regimes across Africa, Latin America, and Southeast Asia represent attempts to sway political allegiances and propagate anti-capitalist ideologies, pushing educational practices and philosophies that are fundamentally at odds with the principles that have defined our progress. If we fail to challenge these efforts head-on, we risk a severe decline in living standards, a stifling of innovation and progress, and the eventual concentration of power and wealth in an elite governing class.

The press, often referred to as the "fourth estate," plays a vital and irreplaceable role in the health of our democracy. A free and independent press, as guaranteed by our Constitution, is a privilege that many in the world cannot claim. However, this privilege comes with a profound responsibility: to provide fair, unbiased, and investigative reporting that is untainted by the priorities of the news organizations themselves. The erosion of objectivity, the suppression of dissenting voices, and the growing blur between fact and opinion pose existential threats to the very foundation of our democratic system. We must demand a return to the cherished principles of journalism: to educate, to challenge, and, most importantly, to distinguish truth from falsehood. The press must never become the arbiter of policy direction—such decisions belong exclusively to the electorate. Unfortunately, the retreat from journalistic ethics began with the reduction in the number of primary news outlets and the consolidation of media ownership, whether in print, radio, or television. This trend has significantly diminished competition. Thankfully, the growth of social media platforms provides new opportunities to share diverse viewpoints, allowing for a more dynamic exchange of ideas.

Our educational system must evolve to meet the demands of the 21st century. The increasing diversity of students, the expanding range of career opportunities, and the growing recognition of the various learning styles students bring with them all necessitate a reimagining of how we approach education. It is no longer enough to simply transmit knowledge;

we must foster critical thinking, champion STEM and STEAM education, and ensure a deep understanding of history through innovative teaching methods. The changing global environment requires a responsive, adaptive educational system. We must stand firm against the rewriting of history and the imposition of politically motivated curricula. The future of our country hinges on the ability of an educated citizenry to navigate the complexities of an ever-changing world, equipped with the knowledge, skills, and discernment to shape it.

The future of America is in our hands. Government, the press, and education must rise to meet the challenges of our time, embracing innovation while rejecting complacency. We must honor the legacy of the nation's founders and the leaders who have followed, safeguarding the principles that have made America a beacon of liberty and opportunity for the world. Together, we can build a future worthy of our past—a future that will serve not only our generation but also generations to come.

Epilogue

"Gratitude makes sense of our past, brings peace for today, and creates a vision for tomorrow."
— *Melody Beattie, Self-Help Author*

Each generation is unique in its own right, and Baby Boomers are no exception. We are the heirs to the "greatest generation," those who made immense sacrifices to preserve our nation and to provide a better life for future generations. The Baby Boomer generation acts as the bridge between two distinct eras—those of our parents and our children and grandchildren. The world as we know it would be unrecognizable to our grandparents. We have experienced the tail end of the Korean War, lived through the protests of the Vietnam War, and ushered in the information age, which continues to reshape our economy and culture, replacing a once-dominant manufacturing ethos.

When I first shared the idea for this writing project with a colleague from Kiwanis, he asked me what I had learned throughout this process. The experiences I've highlighted in these pages have been deeply influential in shaping the life of this 'boomer,' and they provide a clear answer to that question. The central themes that have emerged underscore three guiding principles that have shaped my life: faith, people, and responsibility. These principles, when combined with my love for the United States and my desire to explore the world, have defined me.

Throughout my journey, I have felt the guiding hand of God—often in ways that were invisible to me at the time. His grace has been evident, even when I didn't understand its importance in my early years. Growing up, I didn't fully grasp the significance of the foundation for my faith laid by my parents. Like many teenagers, my involvement in religious activities waned, but it was rekindled in my late teens as I began to understand the true meaning of Christmas. Over time, my faith deepened, particularly when my future wife and I attended church together in my early twenties. As my children grew and participated in Sunday school, I too joined an adult class that allowed me to exchange thoughts and ideas with others at various stages of their faith journeys. This exchange of ideas provided the confidence I needed to step into the role of a lay speaker, delivering the Sunday message when asked by the pastor. The process of preparing those sermons, researching scripture, and interacting with diverse Christian writings has profoundly shaped my beliefs and led me to influential figures such as Max Lucado, Norman Vincent Peale, Dietrich Bonhoeffer, and Billy Graham. These authors are among my most trusted resources when I seek a deeper understanding of both scripture and life's larger philosophies.

Max Lucado's writings focus on the power of daily kindness, the importance of gratitude, and overcoming past failures. His work encourages readers to apply these principles to their own lives, inspiring a sense of purpose and fulfillment. Norman Vincent Peale's teachings emphasize the advantages of maintaining a positive mindset, underscoring how optimism improves mental health and resilience. He advocates that facing each challenge with hope and positivity can transform one's entire perspective. It is disheartening to think of those who begin their days filled with negativity, unknowingly setting a discouraging tone for the hours ahead. A pessimistic outlook clouds one's ability to find joy or opportunity in life's challenges.

Dietrich Bonhoeffer is a towering figure of faith. He believed in the inherent goodness of God, the strength of faith, and the presence of God in our lives—even during times of profound suffering. His writings offer a deep spiritual insight, especially his steadfast commitment to these beliefs while imprisoned by Nazi authorities during World War II. Billy Graham, a close contemporary of Bonhoeffer, began his ministry in 1947. Over the course of the next seventy years, Graham's powerful voice reached millions, teaching the importance of prioritizing Christ in one's life. His messages, often accompanied by inspirational music, resonated deeply, leaving an indelible mark on the hearts of many.

The philosophies I have absorbed from these authors have led me to believe that God's purpose for each individual extends beyond the limitations of time and space. It is woven into the relationships we build throughout our lives. Human connections are vital to our existence, and I have been continuously humbled by the support, love, and guidance I have received from countless individuals. These include my parents, who provided the foundation for my growth; my grandparents and in-laws, who reinforced essential values; and my three sisters, each of whom has been a unique source of strength and encouragement throughout my life. My friends from all walks of life—whether from school, college, or professional settings—have helped sustain me in ways they may not even realize.

Of course, the most important person in my life is my partner, Vickie. Life changed in 1968, and our adventure has continued ever since. Your unwavering spiritual influence and your deep love for children have made all the difference. You have devoted yourself entirely to raising our children, and your grandchildren intuitively respond to your boundless affection. I am forever grateful for your patience and understanding, particularly during the times when my business ventures may have kept me away from home too often. Your support, especially during our time in Kiwanis, which took us to far-off lands and introduced us to countless people, has enriched our lives in ways words cannot capture.

Faith, people, and responsibility form the bedrock of a rewarding life. The responsibility we bear—to God, to family, to country, and to community—must be acknowledged and embraced by each of us. We were not placed in isolation but within a community where we can learn from others and, in turn, contribute to the growth of those around us. Those who live by personal responsibility serve as beacons to those who are still finding their way. I have tried my best to live a responsible life, and I will leave it to others to judge my success.

To my children and grandchildren, as you read these pages, I hope you find nuggets of wisdom that will contribute to your own success. Remember to focus on the goodness in people, nurture your faith, accept your responsibility, and cherish the memories we've shared. And to all those who read these pages, may you find an inspiration or passage that brings a smile to your face, or perhaps a memory long buried that brings comfort to your heart.

Acknowledgements

As a non-professional writer, I rely heavily on the support of others to bring this manuscript to life. I am deeply grateful for the following individuals who have helped shape these pages:

- Tony Knoederer, who reviewed my first draft and offered invaluable insights that helped me refine and focus my efforts.
- Shelley Mann, whose assistance with standardizing punctuation and grammar was essential to the clarity of this work.
- Emma Riley, my talented granddaughter, who not only edited but also asked thoughtful questions that prompted me to create more descriptive chapters and a stronger overall narrative.
- Vickie Riley, my wife, whose unwavering support and love have made this journey possible.
- The unnamed editors at Barnes and Noble who, through their experience, helped bring this project to a conclusion.
- Artificial intelligence, which assisted in enhancing my vocabulary and providing more descriptive language, an area I had never explored before.

I am deeply grateful to each of you for the contributions you've made to this work.

www.ingramcontent.com/pod-product-compliance
Lightning Source LLC
Chambersburg PA
CBHW040801150426
42811CB00056B/1112